Easy Home Remodeling

by Richard V. Nunn

Library of Congress Catalog Card Number: 76-21412
ISBN: 0-8487-0405-3

Manufactured in the United States of America

First Printing 1976

Easy Home Remodeling

Editor: Candace Conard Franklin
Cover Photograph: Taylor Lewis
Onsite framing: Baker Enterprises, Inc. and Devon Redding,
                Birmingham, Alabama

Contents

Introduction

The biggest expense in remodeling your home, regardless of the specific project, is the cost of labor. Materials are not inexpensive, but they are not prohibitive in cost. In fact, you may be surprised by the quality of products your remodeling dollar can buy.

Although *Easy Home Remodeling* does include a discussion of materials, the purpose of the book is to help save money you would otherwise spend on the labor. With the basic information provided, you should be able to complete quite a few home remodeling projects.

The basics of remodeling are emphasized throughout the book— building techniques that are well within your skills. Certain jobs, such as building foundation walls, completing complicated electrical hook-ups, and installing difficult plumbing runs, are best left to a professional. *Easy Home Remodeling* sometimes suggests seeking professional help where the techniques involved in the remodeling go beyond the amateur's skills.

The photographs and text conform to standard building techniques. However, your local building codes may vary slightly with some of these methods. Before beginning any remodeling project, check the building codes and ordinances in your area.

Although this check may be time-consuming, the codes are for your protection; they provide standards for building materials and methods, such as concrete, foundation work, plumbing, heating, air conditioning, electrical wiring, and so forth. Local building codes can be found in the building division of the city hall or at the building division of the county courthouse. Sometimes, the building material retailer where you buy materials will be able to help you with codes and ordinances in your area.

If you plan to add a room to you home where foundation walls, framing, roofing, etc., will be involved, consult an architect or building contractor with design expertise. This service will probably add from 5 to 10 percent to your remodeling bill, but the advice can save many dollars in the long run. In fact, through good design you may be able to save enough on materials to pay the architect's fee.

Finally, think through your remodeling project, regardless of how small, before you start work. Have a definite goal in mind; then sketch out the project, check the local codes and ordinances, purchase the necessary materials and let *Easy Home Remodeling* help you make your dream house a reality.

Remodeling Ideas

This is a "wish" book. But instead of merchandise, the book deals with remodeling and home improvement. The "wishes" here can come true, and you do not even need a magic wand; a hammer is a better substitute.

This chapter presents a potpourri of remodeling ideas that you can fit into your home: kitchens, family rooms, attics, and so on. The following chapters offer the necessary basics to help you do the remodeling yourself—and save money.

Any remodeling or home improvement is a great bargain; it usually is easier and less expensive to improve than to move. This is true in the suburbs as well as the city, since you can get more space for your money and, at the same time, take advantage of the established cultural and architectural appeal of a "settled" neighborhood or area.

The photographs in this chapter are intended as "ideas" to spark a responsive remodeling chord in your handyman spirit. They are not intended as remodeling projects per se, although feel free to copy anything you see. What we really want is for you to think about how these ideas can be adapted to your particular housing problem.

For instance, consider that less than thirty years ago, outdoor living and entertaining was almost unheard of. When you wanted to eat outside, the procedure was to cook the food at home, load the food in the trunk of your car, and drive to a public park or picnic area. With the manufacture of barbecue grilles and other outdoor cooking items, the public park has moved into the backyard—your backyard. But, often, this is a problem because backyards have slopes or big ditches, or they are simply not convenient to reach from the back entrance door or an elevated porch.

The solution to this problem could be a deck or patio, which can be terraced, elevated, or set directly on the ground. Access to the outside living area can be made easy by adding a sliding glass door. The area could be further enhanced by adding landscaping touches, fencing, night lighting, and smart outdoor furniture.

The kitchen is another area frequently remodeled. In fact, surveys show that kitchens are the most remodeled room in a home. And, for the most part, kitchens are easy to remodel because you need only two basic building products: cabinets and a floor covering. You can purchase cabinets that are pre-finished and ready to hang in a wide range of prices. Floor covering is manufactured in hundreds of patterns and types, and, usually, it can be installed directly over the old floor in less than one day.

You also have a dividend in attic and basement space. Since the space is already framed, finishing is usually a matter of applying gypsum board to the framing members, covering the floor, adding lighting, and perhaps building a partition wall or two.

Remodeling does not have to be structural. You can work wonders with a gallon of paint or a wallpaper accent or shutters on windows or new tile on a floor or a new lavatory in the bathroom or paneling in the family room. Even a new light fixture in the kitchen or family room can add sparkle to an otherwise drab room setting.

With the photographs and how-to information in *Easy Home Remodeling*—and your dreams—you will quickly find a solution to your special space problem. After you get started with a remodeling project, you will soon find yourself spending many, many happy hours improving that space, not to mention adding more value to your present home.

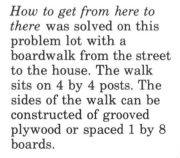

A breakfast/garden room makes this deck more livable in any weather. The room is framed with 2 by 8s and sheathed with plywood. The members were dadoed (notched) to accept the glass, which was set in calking compound to make the glass weather-tight. The floor of the deck serves as the floor in the breakfast room.

How to get from here to there was solved on this problem lot with a boardwalk from the street to the house. The walk sits on 4 by 4 posts. The sides of the walk can be constructed of grooved plywood or spaced 1 by 8 boards.

An attractive wooden bridge provides easy access to backyard activity, which was formerly routed through a garage or kitchen. The span is not long, so you need only two 4 by 4 posts with a 2 by 6 rail.

Far left:
Boardwalk and steps can be a problem solver for uneven lots. The boardwalk here adds architectural interest to the house and yard, besides setting up a patio/deck traffic pattern. The walk is supported by concrete piers set 5 feet apart along the run of the walk. The boards are 2 by 8 cedar, nailed to support runners which sit on the piers. Redwood or cypress could be used for the walk as well as cedar since cedar resists rot from moisture.

Left:
The walk design here utilizes both wood and concrete. The walk is supported by 4 by 4 posts and double 2 by 8s bolted to the posts. The same support idea could be used for a deck where sloping ground is a problem.

An entrance bridge has a definite safety advantage over steps. The deck is supported by 4 by 4 posts resting on piers; the railing, 2 by 6s set on edge, is supported by lengths of square wrought iron.

A low built-in barbecue pit is the focal point on this deck. Otherwise wasted space is utilized by built-in benches. Note how the gate blends in with the decking, which is 2 by 6 cedar.

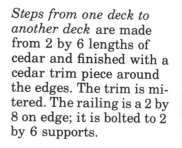

Steps from one deck to another deck are made from 2 by 6 lengths of cedar and finished with a cedar trim piece around the edges. The trim is mitered. The railing is a 2 by 8 on edge; it is bolted to 2 by 6 supports.

This "Florida" room is united with the outside brick patio by using the same brick for the room's floor and the patio. The louvered windows and door also add to the basic design; the horizontal louvers make the room appear longer than it really is.

Outside, the "Florida" room blends in nicely with the architecture of the house. The landscaping is neatly done, not overpowering for the size and shape of the brick patio. The outdoor furniture adds the touch of color necessary to draw the indoors out and make it a single living unit.

A zoned kitchen has an oven/counter work area and follows the triangular principle described in Measuring and Measurements. Stock kitchen cabinets may be used, with the ovens sandwiched between the cabinet modules. The cabinets are fastened to the framing members of the wall with screws.

Although this kitchen is large, a corridor-type plan was used to take advantage of all the floor space possible. The floor is brick to blend with the rest of the home's architecture. Any design floor covering, however, could be used as long as it blends with the wallcovering and window shades.

This galley-type kitchen utilizes shelving, rather than cabinets, to carry out the rustic decorating plan. The ceilings and walls are paneled with real tongue and groove boards in a horizontal configuration; track lighting serves both the kitchen and the dining area. The home office/study center here can be converted into a pantry, depending on your life-style. The floor is cast stone, laid in a bed of mortar; the joints between the stones are struck to give the floor a three-dimensional appearance.

The shelf at the left is adjustable. Notice the countertop which has been extended down one side of the drawer unit to complete the end of the kitchen.

The serving table, like the countertops, is a series of 2- by 3-inch dimension lumber laminated together. Under-the-table stretchers of the same laminated material add stability. The same effect can be created by using high-pressure laminate in a butcher block pattern over 3/4-inch plywood. The stretchers are designed so stools may slip under them, freeing valuable floor space in the kitchen work area.

This live-in kitchen once was a family room. The space now becomes a versatile, hospitable core of the house. The area overlooks a courtyard, and the counter in the background has a built-in grille and bar area.

Right:

The island work table with plenty of illumination from an overhead skylight is the big feature of this kitchen. The range and grille area (not shown) has a brick-arched opening designed to conceal a vent hood. The floor is simulated slate.

Far right:

A breakfast room off the kitchen area takes little space. The kitchen/breakfast area is united by the same sheet vinyl floor covering. Contact paper on the cabinet fronts and columns also help carry the kitchen theme through to the breakfast room.

This family room off the kitchen area was opened up with fixed glass between 4 by 4 framing members on 48-inch centers.

A formal/informal family room takes advantage of wood tones for warmth. The brick fireplace has a rough-sawn mantle, while the bar area has a more formal look. Wood and brick are neatly blended here to carry out the rustic decorating theme. The soffit around the room hides indirect lighting. The floor is simulated pegged oak in strips.

Two rooms were tied together—kitchen and family room—by using the same ceiling tile in both rooms.

Knotty pine paneling can accent a basement room. Here, the paneling was finished with walnut stain varnish to create a "rich" look and blend in with the furnishings in the room.

To redo this dining room, wide-blade plantation shutters were installed at the windows. The shutters frame, but do not block, a view of the garden.

This casual living area off the kitchen was formerly one half of a two-car garage. The television is concealed under the counter of a wet bar at one end of the room. The opening leads to a deck. The same plan could be used for a basement room especially if the basement room opens to the outside.

Far left:
Another room addition has paneling running throughout the walls and ceiling. The floor is simulated brick in a vinyl sheet pattern. Notice how the area rug pulls in the furnishings, making the area one compact unit.

Left:
The entrance to your home can be highlighted by adding another door, as shown here. The opening is easy to frame by using double jambs and headers.

This addition is a "shed" type structure tacked along one end of the house. For a double entry, a spiral staircase is cleverly utilized. The area is paved with smooth brick set without mortar; the brick adjoins a wooden deck.

Financing a Remodeling Project

You want to remodel the attic or basement or kitchen or bathroom, but there just isn't enough money in the sock to finance the job.

Sound familiar?

Relax. Home improvement loans are relatively easy to obtain. Statistics show that the Federal Housing Administration (FHA) has lost only about 2 percent of its remodeling loans on more than $2 billion loaned since 1934—attractive odds to a financial institution.

For help in financing a remodeling project, consider the following alternatives:

• *Short-term and revolving credit.* If your remodeling job is not going to cost too much (around $700), the building material retailer or home center where you buy remodeling materials will often extend you credit. The revolving credit plan extends the payment period for 30 days, interest free. If you must take more than 30 days to pay, you usually will be charged interest on the balance. Be sure to check out the interest rates; retailers are required by law to tell you the interest rate you will be charged. The interest percentage is usually 1½ percent per month, or 18 percent per year.

Some retailers are now offering a ceiling charge account. With this type of account, you may charge from $300 to $500 and pay it back on an installment plan. Again, the interest is usually 18 percent per year, but be sure to check it out before you sign any agreement.

• *Insurance loans.* You can borrow money on your insurance policy if the policy is current. Insurance companies sometimes will let you borrow up to 95 percent of the *cash value* of the policy; the interest rates run about 6 percent per year. Discuss such loans with your insurance agent.

• *Open-end mortgages.* If you have not yet paid off the mortgage on your home, you may have an open-end clause in the mortgage which allows you to reborrow money equal to the mortgage principal you have paid. In fact, the interest rate on the money may be the same interest you are paying on the mortgage.

• *Conventional home improvement loans.* Many savings and loan associations, banks, mutual savings banks, and commercial banks will lend money on home improvements. This type of loan, however, varies according to the availability of money the lenders have to lend. You can usually gauge the availability of money by advertisements run by finance companies in your local newspaper and on local television and radio.

• *Reworking existing mortgages.* Cash for home improvements is sometimes made available by simply refinancing your present mortgage. The cost of money today may prohibit this move, especially if you have a low interest rate on your present mortgage, but it is still worth checking into, particularly if the improvement loan will be for a large sum of money.

• *Bank loans.* You may be able to borrow money for home improvements from a bank on your signature. Do not consolidate any other loans you might have with a home improvement loan, and *do not* have a contractor place a lien on your property if he arranges financing for you.

• *Credit unions.* If you belong to a

credit union, be sure to ask the director for information on a home improvement loan. Usually, the interest rates are within reason, and there is plenty of time to repay the loan.

• *Finance companies.* Usually, finance companies are the last resort for a home improvement loan. There is nothing wrong with accredited finance companies; it's just that interest rates can be very high, and the repayment arrangements may be difficult to comply with. Have the company answer all your questions satisfactorily before you sign such a loan agreement.

Remodeling contractors

The cost of labor for any remodeling project is staggering. The purpose of *Easy Home Remodeling* is to help you to help yourself and, therefore, to lower these labor costs. Any time you do the painting, put up an accent wall, tape gypsum board joints, lay a floor, install rough electrical wiring or plumbing, you are saving up to $20 per hour, perhaps more.

Should you wish to hire a contractor to do some, or all, of the work, follow these guidelines to help save time and money:

• Get at least three different bids on your remodeling project.

• Check out the three bidding contractors with the local Chamber of Commerce or the Better Business Bureau.

• Do not let a contractor finance the job with a lien on your home.

• Ask for at least five references from the contractor and phone these references. Do not be bashful about doing so.

• Have the contractor give you a written contract including an estimate on the work to be done. *Insist on this.*

• Make sure the cost of the work to be done is the *total* cost.

• Make sure the contractor obtains the proper building permits.

• Have your contractor give you a schedule of the remodeling: the start-ing date and the finishing date. Hold the contractor to this schedule, unless circumstances occur over which the contractor has no control.

• Do not give any contractor money in advance for improvements. The contractor may request installment payments as certain stages of the work are completed. This is an acceptable procedure if the work to that point has been satisfactory. The usual arrangement is one-third the fee when the job is half done, another third on completion, and the balance of the fee when all necessary certificates are obtained from the contractor.

• Have a firm arrangement with the contractor on how payment is to be made, particularly if subcontractors are involved in your project.

• Do not sign any agreement until you have thought it over for at least three days.

• If appliances are involved in the remodeling, always obtain the manufacturers' warranties and guarantees on the appliances and cabinets, if cabinets are involved. Insist on an owner's manual on all appliances. File these manuals in a safe place; they can save you money on service calls later.

• If you do the work yourself, make sure that you follow strictly the building codes in your area. Check the codes with your building material or home-center retailer, or the municipal building department in your town. If you hire a contractor, the contractor should obtain the proper building permits. Make sure you see these permits before the contractors starts work.

• Before starting any electrical or plumbing job on your own, be sure you have the necessary expertise. Only the basics are included in *Easy Home Remodeling;* you must have some working knowledge of electricity and plumbing before attempting those areas of remodeling.

Basic Tools and Fasteners

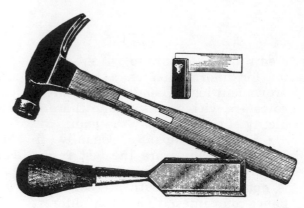

You will need a few basic hand tools to do remodeling work. You may also need specialized tools for such projects as concrete finishing, electrical work, and plumbing; tools and materials for these projects are under the appropriate chapter.

Tools

For general remodeling work you will need these basic tools:
- 13-ounce claw hammer
- Crosscut saw
- Rip saw
- Miter box and backsaw
- Block lane
- Carpenter's square
- Spirit level
- Plumb bob
- Chalk line and chalk
- Nail set
- Screwdriver set (standard and Phillips head)
- Chisel set
- Putty knife
- Wall scraper

The total cost of these basic tools should run about $110. Purchase quality tools; they will last a lifetime if you take care of them, and they cost only a few dollars more than lower grade tools. Quality tools are also safer to use than the cheap counterparts because they are properly balanced and keep their sharp edges longer.

Fasteners

In all phases of remodeling you will need nails, screws, glue, and other types of fasteners; sizes and types, of course, depend on the project at hand.

Nails

Nails are specified by inches and "penny" sizes. The penny size (which also refers to length) is noted by the letter d. A 5-penny nail, for example, is specified as $5d$ on the package and is 1¾ inches long. The diameter (gauge) of the nail almost always increases with the length of the nail. Nails, such as floor brads, for special jobs are manufactured in only one size. Shingle nails are made in only one diameter, but in several lengths.

The nail size you use should be three times longer than the thickness

Common nail sizes		
d or Penny size	Length (inches)	Gauge (diameter)
2	1	15
3	1¼	14
4	1¼	12½
5	1¾	12½
6	2	11½
7	2¼	11½
8	2½	10¼
9	2¾	10¼
10	3	9
12	3¼	9
16	3½	8
20	4	6
30	4¼	5
40	5	4
50	5¼	3
60	6	2

of the board or lumber you are nailing. If you are working with thin and thick pieces of material, such as ¼-inch thick plywood and 2- by 4-inch framing, always try to fasten the thin piece to the thicker piece so that two-thirds of the nail will be in the thicker piece. Nails hold best when they are driven into the wood at a slight angle.

Nails are manufactured from aluminum, copper, brass, stainless steel, bronze, and Monel metal. Common nails are used for framing or rough-in carpentry jobs; finishing nails are for trim and cabinet projects. Casing nails are similar to finishing nails, but are heavier in body. Ring or ring-shanked nails are for extra holding power.

Nails are sold by the box or pound (actual pound weight) at building material retail outlets, hardware stores, home-center stores, and general merchandise stores.

Screws

Like nails, the screws you use to fasten materials together should be three times longer than the thickness of the material. Screw sizes are numbered according to the length and gauge (thickness). A No. 16 wood screw, for example, is 2½ inches long. Lengths range from ¼ inch to 6 inches; the sizes are usually approximate.

Screw types include oval head and flathead screws, which are countersunk (recessed) below the surface of the material, and roundhead screws, which are not countersunk. There are two basic slot types: plain slotted, which requires a standard blade screwdriver, and Phillips slotted, for which you use a Phillips screwdriver.

You can purchase decorative washers for those screws that will show on cabinets. Washers also provide more bearing surface for the screwheads and help prevent marring of the wood when the screws are driven or drawn.

Other fasteners

Toggle bolts and molly anchors. Many remodeling projects call for two types of fasteners, toggle bolts and molly anchors, which are used to attach furring strips and cabinets to hollow walls (the space between the studs). Both fasteners are manufactured in a wide range of screw diameters and lengths.

Masonry anchor and lag bolts. If you plan to fasten framing to a concrete floor, choose masonry anchors, lag bolts with lead expansion anchors, or concrete nails. You have to drill a

Common screw sizes			
Gauge	*Length*	*Gauge*	*Length*
No. 2	¼ to ½ inch	No. 10	⅝ to 2¼ inches
No. 3	¼ to ⅝ inch	No. 12	⅞ to 2½ inches
No. 4	⅜ to ¾ inch	No. 14	1 to 2¾ inches
No. 5	⅜ to ¾ inch	No. 16	1¼ to 3 inches
No. 6	⅜ to 1½ inches	No. 18	1½ to 4 inches
No. 7	⅜ to 1½ inches	No. 20	1¾ to 4 inches
No. 8	½ to 2 inches	No. 24	3½ to 4 inches
No. 9	⅝ to 2¼ inches		

hole in the concrete for masonry anchors. When you twist in the lag bolts, these anchors expand in the hole in the concrete and grip the edges of the hole; this holds the sill or plate tightly against the concrete floor. Masonry anchors also may be used in reinforced concrete walls, concrete block walls, and brick walls.

Adhesives. Glue or other adhesives are fasteners you will use often in remodeling. The adhesive chart in this chapter will help you decide on the type to buy.

When using any adhesive on wood joints, be sure to sand the joints lightly before you apply the adhesive. Sanding opens the pores of the wood so that the adhesive sticks better. All wood joints should be perfectly square; the more gluing surface, the better the glue holds.

Clamp all joints if possible when gluing, but do not clamp the wood too tightly or the adhesive will be squeezed out of the joint. Finger-tight pressure on the clamp is usually best. A filler-type glue may be used when clamps cannot be used.

Always read the label on glue containers, and follow the manufacturer's directions for mixing and applying the adhesive. Drying time is affected by humidity; but, in general, fast drying time is 1 hour, and a medium length of drying time is 2 hours.

Abrasives

All remodeling projects call for an abrasive: sandpaper.

Adhesives

Type of adhesive	Drying time	Use	Data
Aliphatic resin	Fast	Wood	Water resistant; use with lacquer finishes.
Casein	Medium	Wood Fabrics	Good heat resistance; poor water resistance.
Casein or latex	Medium	Metal Glass Fabric Plastic	Good heat resistance; good water resistance; dries clear.
Thermoplastic	Fast	Wood Paper Fabrics	May damage rubber, plastic, lacquer finishes.
Thermosetting	Medium	Wood Paper Fabrics	Won't stain.
Contact	Fast	Wood Paper Fabrics Laminates	High heat resistance; must work quickly since adhesive dries fast.
Epoxy	Medium	Wood Metal	Expensive; excellent holding ability.

Abrasives are classified as "open coat" and "closed coat." This means that the abrasive is adhered to the backing in a "spaced out" (open) configuration, or the abrasive is "close together" (closed). An open coat abrasive will not "fill" with residue as quickly as a closed coat abrasive.

Abrasives are fixed to a backing of either paper or cloth. The backing weight is specified by letter: *A* for lightweight, *D* for heavyweight, *J* for lightweight on a cloth backing, and *X* for heavyweight on a cloth backing.

Standard abrasives usually are specified by number or letter. Very fine abrasive paper is rated from 220 to 600; fine is rated from 120 to 180;

medium is rated from 50 to 100; coarse is rated from 36 to 40; and very coarse is rated from 12 to 30.

Aluminum oxide abrasive is a good choice for smoothing wood and plastics. It cuts fast, and you can use it a long time before it wears out.

Silicon carbide abrasive is tough and may be used for sanding very hard plastics, glass, and ceramic surfaces.

Garnet abrasive is used for wood.

Emery abrasive is used for wood; it wears out rapidly.

Flint abrasive is inexpensive. It is used for smoothing wood that is full of sap or for smoothing painted surfaces. Flint paper wears out rapidly.

Abrasive papers			
Aluminum oxide *Silicon carbide* *Garnet*	*Emery*		*Flint*
Very fine	600 500 400 (10/0) 360 320 (9/0) 280 (8/0) 240 (7/0) 220 (6/0)		Very fine
Fine	180 (5/0) 150 (4/0) 120 (3/0)	3/0 2/0 1/0	Fine
Medium	100 (2/0) 80 (1/0) 60 (½)	½ 1 1½	Medium
Coarse	50 (1) 40 (1½) 36 (2)	2 2½ 3	Coarse
Very coarse	30 (2½) 24 (3) 20 (3½) 16 (4) 12 (4½)		Very coarse

Materials

Most remodeling projects require the same basic materials. These materials include boards, lumber, plywood, hardboard, moldings and trim, and gypsum wallboard.

Lumber and boards

There are two classifications of lumber and boards: softwood and hardwood. Softwoods—hemlock, fir, pine, spruce—are used for framing remodeling projects. Hardwood—mahogany, walnut, oak, maple—usually are specified for cabinets, flooring, and trim. Hardwoods are more expensive than softwoods, so plan carefully where you will use them.

Dimension lumber is lumber that is 2 inches thick in nominal size (as it comes from the sawmill). When you purchase 2 by 4s, 2 by 6s, and 2 by 8s, you are buying *dimension* lumber.

Boards are 1 inch thick in nominal size. For example, 1 by 2s, 1 by 4s, and 1 by 6s are classed as *boards*. Although you order and buy the lumber and boards according to their nominal size, the actual size—after shrinking and planing—is what you take home. (See size chart.)

Boards and lumber are especially graded according to two basic classifications: *common lumber*, which has defects and is used for construction and general-purpose building projects such as framing, and *select lumber*, which is sound and of good quality, and is used when appearance is important.

The grades of common lumber are: No. 1, which contains only a few tight knots and blemishes and is suitable for painting; No. 2, which has larger knots and blemishes and can also be painted or used for flooring and paneling; No. 3, which has loose knots and flaws and should be used for shelving or where the wood will not show; and No. 4, which is an economy grade and should be used only for subflooring, crating, sheeting, and concrete forms.

The grades of select lumber are: B and Better (or 1 and 2 clear), which has only tiny imperfections; C select grade, which has limited imperfections; D select grade, which has many imperfections and is sometimes sold covered by a coat of paint to hide the defects.

Lumber and boards are sold by the board foot. A board foot is a piece of lumber that is 1 inch thick, 12 inches wide, and 12 inches long. Building material retailers will compute the measurements for you.

Basic lumber and board sizes

Lumber type	Nominal size (inches)	Actual size (inches) (Material surfaced four sides and kiln dried)
Boards	1x2	¾x1½
	1x3	¾x2½
	1x4	¾x3½
	1x5	¾x4½
	1x6	¾x5½
	1x7	¾x6½
	1x8	¾x7½
Dimension	2x4	1½x3½
	2x6	1½x5½
	2x8	1½x7¼
	2x10	1½x9¼

Plywood sheets

Plywood sheets are available in two faces: hardwood-faced and softwood-faced. Hardwood faces include oak, mahogany, cherry, birch, and walnut; softwood faces include fir, pine, and spruce.

Most plywood is subject to industry grading standards which assure consumers that the material purchased is uniform. There are standards that permit plugging knotholes and mending split voids, but this does not mean that the material is of inferior quality; instead, it assures that you get what you pay for.

Most plywood which is readily available today is graded by the American Plywood Association and bears a back stamp or edgemark on the panel. This mark is your assurance that the plywood has been manufactured to the quality standards and performance requirements of the Association.

The following grading information is designed to give you an understanding of plywood when talking to your plywood dealer. With this help you can select the plywood best suited to your project and your budget.

Hardwood-faced plywood

Graded differently from the softwood-faced, hardwood-faced plywood comes in interior type, which is moisture resistant, and exterior type, which is waterproof.

Hardwood-faced plywood is further defined according to veneer grades: the better the grade, the more expensive the material. These grades include:

  A Premium
  1 Good
  2 Sound
  3 Utility
  4 Backing
  SP Specialty grade (which has unusual decorative features)

Hardwood-faced plywood is used primarily as paneling or as facing material in the ¼-inch thickness and for construction of furniture or cabinets in the ¾-inch thickness; it is often prefinished. Hardwood-faced plywood is sometimes available with matching trim and colored nails are available to fasten the trim to furring strips and subframing.

Although you can build cabinets from hardwood-faced plywood, you might consider a less expensive frame with a hardwood facing, or use softwood-faced plywood, which is usually less expensive, and apply your own finish.

Softwood-faced plywood

Softwood-faced plywood is also manufactured in exterior and interior types. These two types are further identified according to appearance by veneer grades, and according to stiffness and strength by groups.

Exterior plywood is waterproof and is suited to permanent outdoor applications and to those items subject to constantly moist conditions or extremely high humidity. Interior plywood is highly moisture resistant and is well-suited for storage.

Veneer grades are designed according to the appearance quality of the face and back veneer, and are coded with letters:

N Special order "natural finish" veneer; select all hardwood or all sapwood; free of open defects; allows some repairs. (This grade is in limited supply and is very expensive.)

A Smooth and paintable; neatly made repairs permissable.

B Solid surface veneer; circular and other nontapered repair plugs and tight knots permitted.

C Knotholes and limited splits permitted; minimum veneer permitted in exterior-type plywood.

C-Plugged Improved *C* veneer with splits limited to ⅛ inch in width and knotholes and borer holes limited to ¼ inch by ½ inch.

D Permits knots and knotholes to 2½ inches in width and ½ inch larger under certain specified limits; limited splits permitted.

Where the plywood will show, consider *A* or *B* veneers; when appearance is not important, use *C*, *C-plugged*, or *D*.

Softwood-faced plywood is designated by group to indicate its stiffness and strength and the species of wood it contains. The groups range from 1 through 5 with the stiffest and strongest woods in Group 1.

Similarities between hardwood-faced and softwood-faced plywoods include grade combinations, glue bonds, and thicknesses. You can buy veneer grade combinations so that when the face will show and the backing will not show, you can choose a 1 front and a 3 back in hardwood-faced plywood or an *A* front and *C* back in softwood-faced plywood. In general, the glue bonds of both faces are classified as waterproof, water resistant, and dry. Even if you purchase an interior plywood (hardwood- or softwood-faced), you may want a waterproof bond if the plywood is being used in a spot with high humidity. Thicknesses of hardwood-faced and softwood-faced plywood are ¼, ⅜, ½, ⅝, ¾, and 1 inch.

Hardboard sheets

Hardboard is really wood. The material is made from wood chips that are turned into sheets under heat and pressure.

There are two types of hardboard: standard and tempered. If moisture is not a problem, use standard; tempered hardboard has been specially treated to withstand moisture.

Hardboard makes excellent sliding cabinet doors, drawer bottoms, floor underlayment, and decorative inserts. It is less expensive than plywood.

When working with hardboard, remember that it is grainless. Therefore, hardboard has to be fastened to wood framing members. You cannot fasten the wood to hardboard. Do not nail or screw a piece of trim to the hardboard; nail or screw the hard-

board to the trim.

Sizes of hardboard panels range from 4 by 4 to 4 by 16 feet. The standard sizes are 4- by 8- and 4- by 10-foot panels. Thicknesses are ⅛, ³⁄₁₆, ¼, and ⁵⁄₁₆ inch.

There is a wide range of hardboard panels with embossed designs. The embossing is so realistic that it is difficult to tell the product from real hardwood-faced plywood. You may be able to use these panels to face some storage projects and for wall paneling, always fastening the hardboard to a framework.

Hardboard manufacturers also provide various molding and trim for their products. The moldings usually are metal with an embossed covering, and nails are available that match the panel and the molding finish.

Working with hardboard and plywood

Special tools are not necessary to work with plywood or hardboards, but consider these tips to make sawing, smoothing, and planing easier.

• Cut plywood with a crosscut saw. Turn the best side of the panel up, and support the panel with sawhorses or a sturdy table so the saw does not bind in the kerf.

• If you cut plywood with a power saw, turn the best side of the panel down. Use a crosscut blade or a combination blade on the saw.

• When planing plywood, start from the ends and run the plane toward the center of the panel to prevent splitting at corners and edges.

• Always sand plywood in the direction of the grain. Stretch the sandpaper over a sanding block, and do not apply too much pressure, which tends to "dig" the top veneer, and do not sand too much, which can cut through the thin top veneer.

• If possible, never drive a nail or screw into the edge of plywood; this can split the veneer. If you have to use a fastener in an edge, drill a pilot hole for the fastener.

• If you are paneling a room with plywood, separate and lean the panels against the walls of the room for several days. This permits the wood to adjust to the humidity in the room. Low and high humidity can shrink and swell the panels so there are cracks between the joints after application.

• Saw hardboard with a crosscut saw. If you use a power saw, use a combination or crosscut blade, or a carbide-tipped blade. Hardboard is extremely dense and this toughness dulls sawblades quickly.

• When drilling holes in hardboard, work from the "finished" side of the sheet.

• Hardboard must be supported by framing members such as 2 by 4s. In installations where panels are used, support the panels every 16 inches.

• Before installing hardboard, or plywood in damp exterior conditions, cover the walls adjoining the panels with a moisture-vaporproof barrier such as polyethylene film.

• Hardboard panels, such as those used in drawer bottoms, should "float." Do not fasten the panels securely; hardboard tends to absorb moisture and expand. Leave a little space for this expansion and the contraction that may later result.

Moldings and trim

Molding patterns, including trim, are so varied that a list here would be impossible. The ones you will be interested in include crown, cove, quarter round, baseboard and shoe, and half round.

Moldings and trim are purchased by the linear foot; the configuration of the material will determine the price. For this reason, crown molding is more expensive than quarter round.

Gypsum wallboard

This material has a gypsum core covered on both sides with a paper

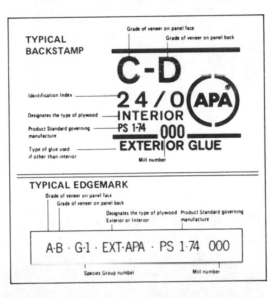

Plywood grade stamps on the face or edges of the panels look like this. All panels approved by the American Plywood Association carry the stamping.

Veneer-core plywood has a series of inner plies. The top and bottom veneers are bonded to these plies under great pressure. The wood grain in the veneers are alternated at right angles during manufacture to give the panels more strength. For constructing exterior storage areas, sheathing, etc., use exterior-type plywood; for interior projects, use interior-type plywood with a water-resistant bond.

material. It is an innovative replacement for lath and plaster and may be used for both wall and ceiling coverings.

Standard gypsum wallboard sizes include panels from 4 feet wide to 16 feet long. Typical sizes are 4 by 8 and 4 by 10 feet. Thicknesses range from ¾ to ½ to ⅝ inches. The ⅝-inch thickness is best for most remodeling projects.

Gypsum wallboard is available with edges that have a slight taper to them, letting you fit the joint tape flush over the panel. You also may buy other edge treatments including round, beveled, eased, square, and tongue and groove. These panels, however, usually have to be special ordered. Some panels are decorated; others are coated with a moisture-resistant paper/sealer. These special features make the wallboard more expensive than regular gypsum board.

Particle board-core plywood is either veneered on both sides of the core or veneered on just one side. The other side is sanded smooth. Particle board is also available without veneer. This product is good for floor underlayment and sub-flooring. Particle board is manufactured from wood chips that are resin coated; the board is very dense and heavy. Like hardboard, particle board should be nailed to framing members. Do not nail the framing members to it unless the particle board has a veneer surface finish. Particle board is dimensionally stable and is a good choice for such projects as cabinets.

Lumber-core plywood has sheets of veneer laminated to a core of solid wood and is especially suited for cabinets, since the core is extremely strong and laminated for stress. The edges of lumber-core plywood are very easy to finish and take mortising and fasteners better than veneer-core or particle board-core panels. You may have to special order lumber-core plywood.

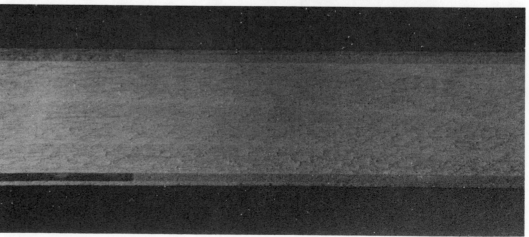

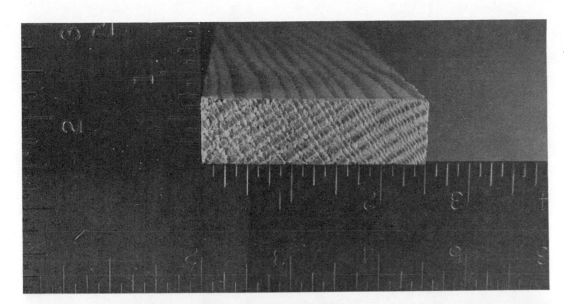

Nominal sizes of boards are 1 by 2, 1 by 3, 1 by 4, etc. The actual size, however, is smaller. Here is a piece of 1 by 3. The actual dimensions are ¾ inch thick by 2½ inches wide.

Dimension lumber also has a nominal size standard. This is a piece of 2 by 4, but the actual dimensions are 1½ inches thick by 3½ inches wide. The "decrease" in size, according to tests run on the materials, does not affect the strength of the boards or lumber.

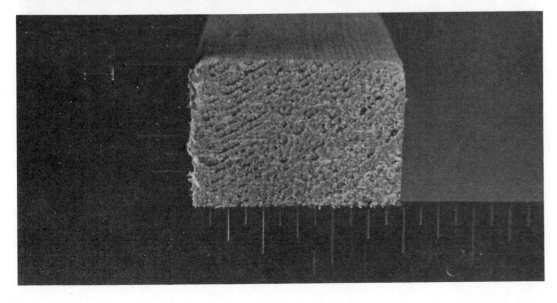

"Full size" lumber also is available at some building material outlets. A piece of 1- by 1½-inch stock is shown here. Some boards and lumber comes rough sawn—it is not surfaced or planed on all four sides. Most boards and dimension lumber you will be working with in remodeling will be specified "S4S." This simply means that the stock is "surfaced four sides."

Flat-grained boards and dimension lumber are stronger than vertical-grained counterparts. The grain of the wood runs across the width of the stock. If you can, select such flat-grained material for framing.

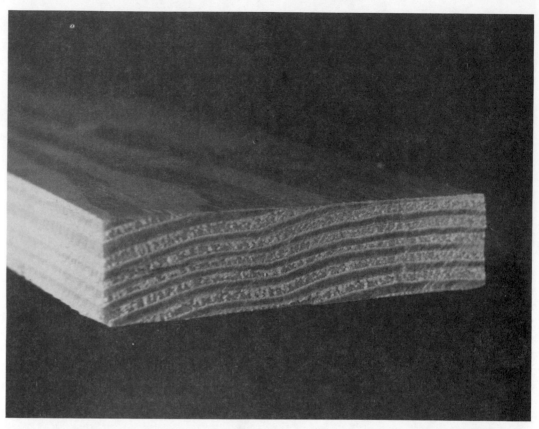

Although flat-grained boards and dimension lumber are stronger than vertical-grained material (shown), they may warp and shrink when exposed to a lot of moisture and humidity. If possible, buy kiln-dried boards and lumber for remodeling jobs. This material may cost a bit more, but it tends to remain stable without developing checks or splitting, bowing, twisting, and cupping.

Measuring
and Measurements

Since remodeling projects vary among readers, the information in this chapter deals with dimension basics to help determine the size project best suited to the available space in your particular home. Framing basics appear in a later chapter; both chapters interrelate.

The most critical part of any remodeling or building project is measuring and marking. *Square, level,* and *plumb* are the three magic words to remember when measuring and marking. The boards and other materials that you cut must be square. The framing that you assemble must be square, level, and plumb. The following tools are necessary for determining square, level, and plumb:

- Carpenter's square
- Spirit level
- Plumb bob and chalk line
- An accurate flexible tape measure

These are the basic measuring and marking tools. Other tools may also prove helpful:

- Combination square
- Try square
- Marking gauge
- Dividers or a compass

The cost of all this equipment is less than $50. Be sure to purchase quality tools; cheap measuring and marking tools can cost time and money in mismarked materials. Do not use a wooden yardstick to measure space; the correct tool to use is an accurate flexible rule.

A wise old carpenter reportedly once said: "Measure twice, cut once." To that statement might well be added, "and save time and money." When you miscut a piece of material, you have lost the price of the material plus the time you spent purchasing and miscutting it.

Manufacturers' literature

Your remodeling project may call for new kitchen cabinets, a new entrance to your home, a new bathroom arrangement, or basement paneling.

Manufacturers' literature is often overlooked in dimension planning. Most building material retailers and home-center stores have a wealth of this literature, which will provide you with hundreds of dimensions of various products such as doors, windows, bathtubs, lavatories, paneling, floor tile, ceramic tile, pipe and tubing, electrical supplies—you name it.

Before making any buying decisions, take a look at this literature. It can help you make a better selection of products, and, in fact, it may help you with any special design problems you might have.

Another good source of dimension planning literature is general merchandise catalogs such as those published by Montgomery Ward and Sears, Roebuck and Co. In addition, do not overlook specialized publications you can purchase on the newsstand. There are hundreds of these magazines that emphasize remodeling projects for bathrooms, attics, basements, kitchens, decks, and patios.

Finally, keep in mind that building materials are based on a module. Therefore, design is based on a module. For example, studs are set on 16-inch centers and 24-inch centers. So are rafters and joists. This is why plywood is manufactured in 4-foot-wide sheets; to accommodate the 16- and 24-inch centers. Cabinets, appliances, and fixtures of all types are also based on this common building module.

Carpenter's square, sometimes called a framing square or rafter square, may be used for marking large surfaces. The square is specially marked so you can use it to mark for rafter cuts and stair stringer cuts. Usually, this square comes with directions for its use. A try square is a smaller version of a framing square. Use it for squaring ends of short and narrow materials and for marking for joining cuts.

A combination square may be used to square short pieces of material. It is especially useful for squaring ends of dimension lumber.

A *spirit level, or carpenter's level,* is used for determining plumb, vertical level, and horizontal level. Simply place the level on the work and read the bubble. When the bubble is between the lines, as shown, the work is plumb or level. Carpenters' levels come with at least three bubbles, one in the center of the level and one at either end. The center bubble is used for locating horizontal level; the end bubbles are used for determining plumb or vertical level.

Levels are available in many lengths and weights. You can also purchase a level that shows elevation and inch rise per foot, but this is really a specialty item, handy when framing a roof, but not a basic tool.

To find a true vertical line on a vertical surface, whether that surface is perpendicular or not, position the flat side of the level on the surface and center the two end bubbles.

To find a true plumb on a vertical surface—to determine whether that surface is perfectly perpendicular—position the edge of the level on the surface, and center the two end bubbles between the lines.

Right:

A *plumb bob* is a pointed weight that is fastened to a stout piece of twine or a chalk line. For illustrative purposes, the line here is shorter than would normally be the case. A plumb bob usually is a framing tool, designed to establish vertical (plumb) lines. Use a plumb bob in conjunction with a framing square and/or level to make sure the line is true.

Far right:

A *chalk line* is a heavy piece of twine coated with (usually) blue chalk and used for marking vertical lines. When the line is leveled (or plumbed) along a flat surface, pulled tight, and snapped, it leaves a chalk mark on the surface. The chalk line may be used on either horizontal or vertical surfaces. You may also use a chalk line in combination with a plumb bob for true vertical lines along dimension lumber and paneling.

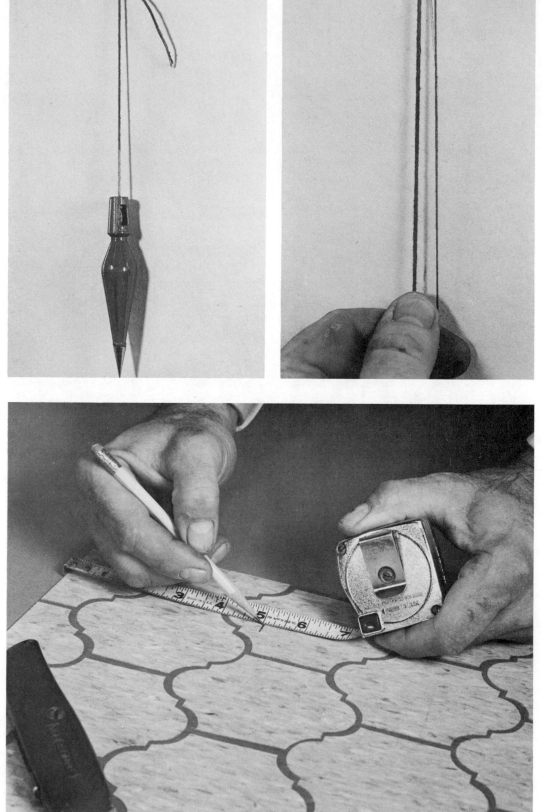

A *flexible tape measure* provides accurate measurements, and you can use the tape to compute the measurements of inside and outside curves. Quality tapes are stiff enough to be extended without support up to about 10 feet. Many tape measures come with buttons which, when pushed, hold the tape at the desired mark. Keep the rule lightly oiled.

Dividers or a compass is a tool for use in scribing circles and duplicating odd shapes for trimming and cutting. For example, to cut a tile to fit around a pipe, press one leg of the divider or compass against the pipe flange (protruding rim on the shaft) and mark this configuration on the tile. The measurement to the tile is its distance to the wall. The dividers or compass has to be set to this measurement. Both tools also may be used to mark off a series of lines along a marked cutting line.

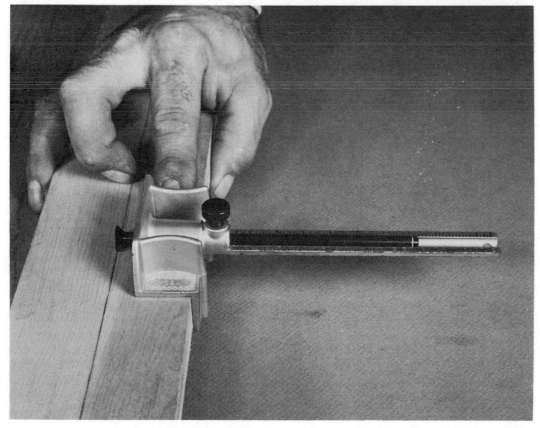

A marking gauge is used to mark cutting lines (with the grain) on boards that have a squared edge. Rule gradations on the gauge provide a guide for the depth of the cut, and the sliding rule is locked into position with a thumbscrew. When using the marking gauge, keep it pressed square against the edge of the material, and apply firm pressure throughout the marking process.

Kitchen floor plans and basic dimensions

Adding a room onto your home or remodeling a basement, attic, or family room in the existing space is not difficult to plan as to space requirements since work surfaces and appliances are not involved. You simply have a certain amount of space to be filled with furniture and storage built-ins.

Kitchen remodeling is different, however. Considerations include special work patterns, appliance placement, and clearances. For best results, design your kitchen remodeling around a triangle plan, as shown in the drawings in this chapter. Always use the kitchen sink as the center point of the triangle. Measurements from this center point to the range and refrigerator should never total less than 12 feet nor more than 22 feet. If the distance is more than this, you will have to take too many steps for efficient food preparation.

You should have at least 1½ feet of counter space beside the refrigerator so that you can easily load and unload the refrigerator without turning to another counter across the room.

Plan on about 2 feet of counter space beside the range. The countertop space should have a wooden insert or be covered with ceramic tile to protect it from hot dishes.

Also in your measurements, allow about 4 feet of additional countertop space for preparing foods. This area should be located near the range or refrigerator, if at all possible. Allow 3 feet of space at each side of the kitchen sink for dirty dishes and food preparation.

If you plan to install a dishwasher in your kitchen remodeling, consider these questions: Do you have a garbage disposer? Do you have a double sink? Are you right- or left-handed? Are there doors of other appliances that might interfere with the positioning of the dishwasher?

Ideally, if you are right-handed, you will work from left to right: scrape the dishes into the disposer, rinse them, and put them into the dishwasher. Therefore, you will want your dishwasher on the right side of the sink. Left-handed people, who work from right to left, should position the dishwasher on the left of the sink. This is the guiding principle to follow, providing that neither the refrigerator door, nor the oven door will in any way obstruct the dishwasher door.

Other considerations:
• Obtain more kitchen efficiency by allowing a space of 3 feet or more between a kitchen cabinet and a doorway.
• Allow 4 feet or more clearance between a cabinet and an opposite appliance.
• Remember that kitchen sinks do not always have to be located under a window.
• Do not place a range under a window.

The U-shape kitchens

This floor plan is the most efficient of the four described here, but you must have enough room to use it—at least an 8-foot width. A narrower space than this causes traffic problems, and only one person can work comfortably within such an area; therefore, a 9- or 10-foot width is best.

In this plan, the kitchen sink is located at the bottom of the U; the range and refrigerator are along the sides of the U. Positive features of the U-shape plan are lack of cross traffic within the space and better storage opportunities.

L-shape kitchens

Space also is needed for this plan which locates the sink on one wall, the range at the bottom of the L, and the refrigerator across from the sink. The L plan takes at least 8 feet of space along each leg of the L. If the space available is less than this figure, consider the U-shape plan. However, you may be able to incorporate some of the

L-shape features into a smaller space, especially if you do not have a lot of appliances.

Features of the *L*-shape kitchen include enough room for kitchen dining, a very smooth traffic flow that permits two cooks in the kitchen at one time, plenty of storage space, and ample space for all major appliances without cutting down on countertop working areas.

The corridor kitchen

This plan calls for the sink to be on one wall and the range and refrigerator on the opposite wall. If you can, try to close one end of the corridor with cabinets, forming a tight *U* shape to make the plan even more efficient.

Do not use the corridor plan if you have less than 5 feet of space between the sink, range, and refrigerator; there would be little room to open the refrigerator door. If space is a prob-lem, try a single wall floor plan that places the sink, range, and refrigerator side-by-side. Folding or narrow countertop space can be designed for the opposite wall.

The island kitchen

You are lucky indeed if you have the space for an island kitchen. At first glance you may think all this space is wasted. It isn't; the island can be used as a countertop range, as an extra countertop working space with storage below, or as a serving table.

An island works best when there is at least 3 feet of walking space between the island and countertops and/or appliances surrounding the island. The working triangle also applies to an island kitchen: the sink positioned in a corner on one wall with the refrigerator near the sink and the range near (or in) the island and close to the sink.

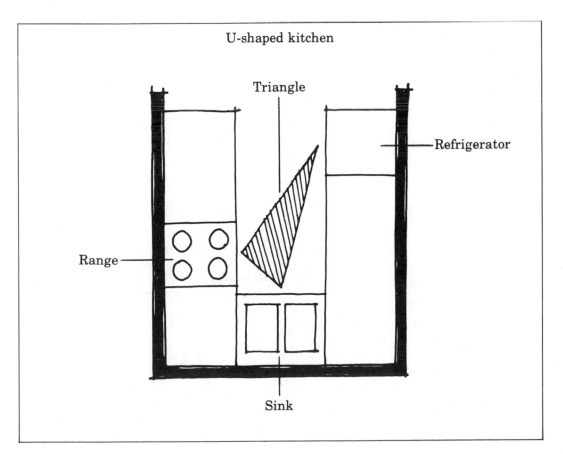

U-shaped kitchen

Triangle

Refrigerator

Range

Sink

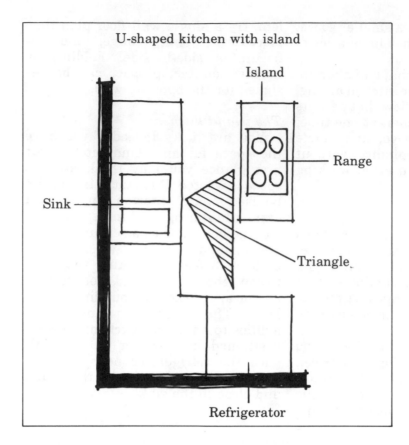

U-shaped kitchen with island

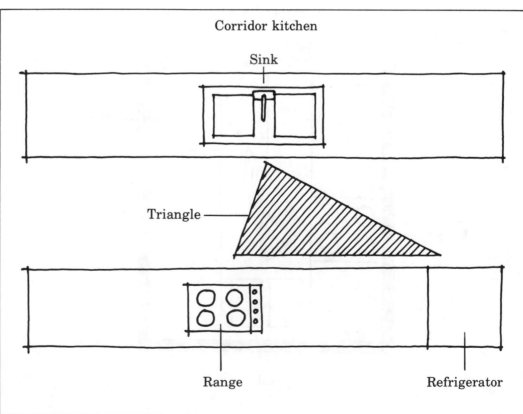

Corridor kitchen

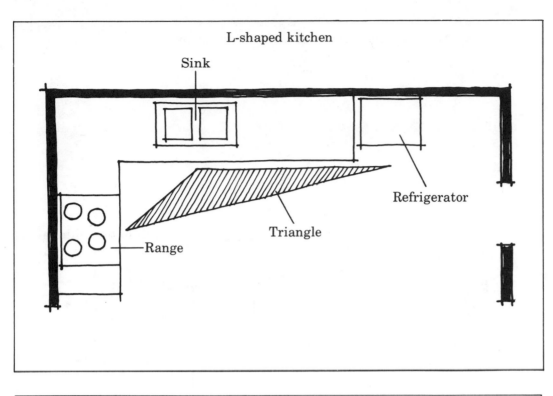

L-shaped kitchen

Sink

Range

Triangle

Refrigerator

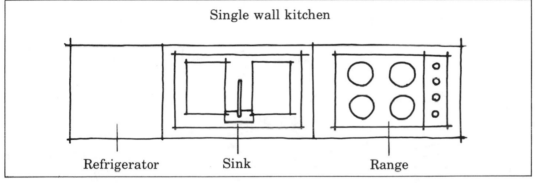

Single wall kitchen

Refrigerator   Sink   Range

Base and wall cabinet dimensions

You can buy stock or ready-made (usually pre-finished) cabinets or custom-built cabinets for your kitchen or bathroom remodeling—or any area where you want cabinet-type storage. Custom-built cabinets are tailored exactly to your space requirements and cost about 10 percent more than stock cabinets.

There is a wide range of wood grains and finishes and prices from which to choose on both stock and custom-built cabinets. The woods include oak, maple, walnut, cherry, pine, pecan, and ash. Or you can pur-chase cabinets that are covered with plastic laminate in wood grain patterns or solid colors. Low-priced units, of course, do not have the workmanship of medium-priced stock or custom-built cabinets.

One of the best guides to selecting cabinets is the National Kitchen Cabinet Association's seal of approval. This seal is attached to both base and wall cabinets, and it is easy to see. The NKCA seal is your assurance that the cabinets have undergone rigid testing for workmanship, use of wood, and finishes.

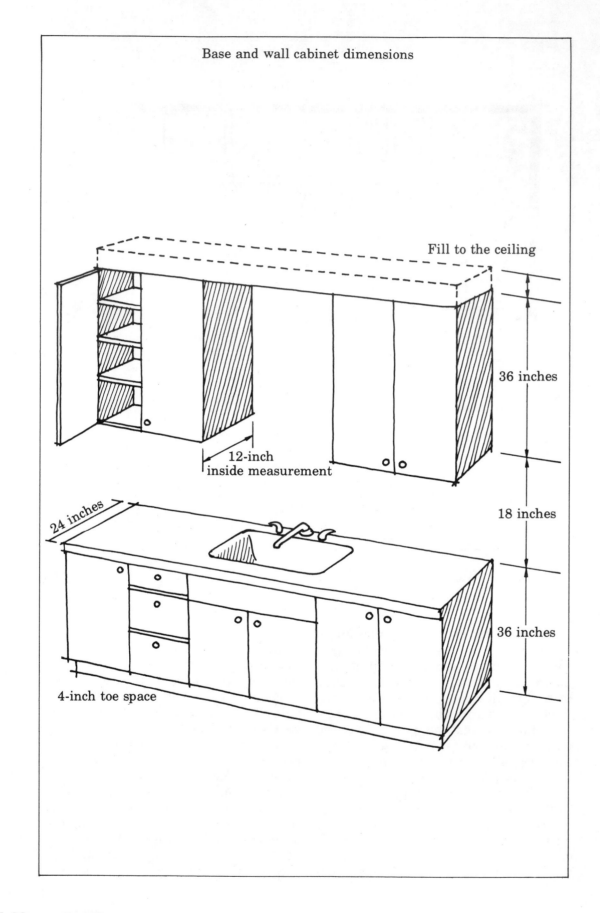

Base and wall cabinet dimensions

Fill to the ceiling

36 inches

12-inch
inside measurement

24 inches

18 inches

36 inches

4-inch toe space

Bookshelves/cabinet dimensions

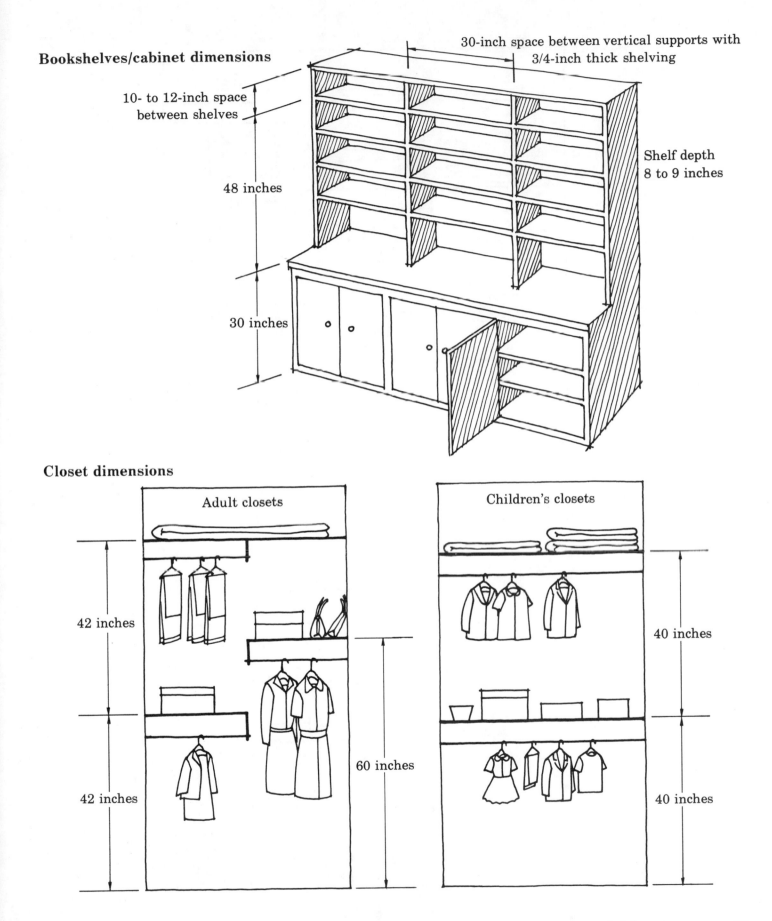

30-inch space between vertical supports with 3/4-inch thick shelving

10- to 12-inch space between shelves

48 inches

30 inches

Shelf depth 8 to 9 inches

Closet dimensions

Adult closets

42 inches

42 inches

60 inches

Children's closets

40 inches

40 inches

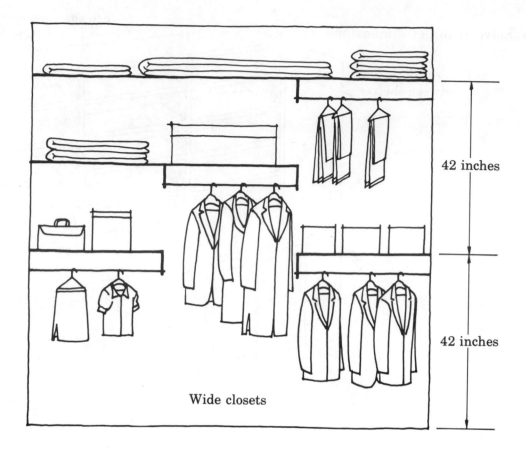

42 inches

42 inches

Wide closets

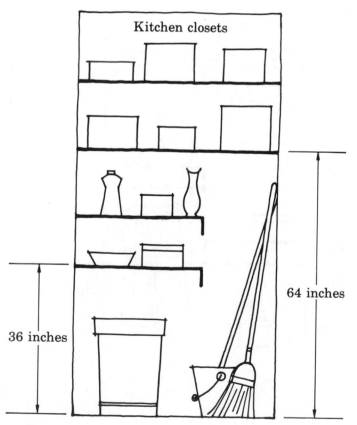

Kitchen closets

64 inches

36 inches

Electrical Basics

When working with anything electrical—remodeling or repairs—there is *one* basic rule that *must* be followed: *Turn off the electricity at the service entry—either a fuse box or circuit breaker.*

You cannot be shocked by electricity when the circuit is defused.

One more caution: Stay in front of the wall when making electrical repairs, unless you are a skilled electrician and unless the building codes in your area permit otherwise. If the job is behind the wall where you cannot see the connection or repair, or if the connection is in a fuse box or circuit breaker or in power supply lines, call in a professional to do the work.

There are three electrical jobs an amateur can do when remodeling:

1. Rough-in wall switches.
2. Rough-in convenience outlets.
3. Connect lighting fixtures; the wiring is contained in metal junction boxes and is accessible.

If you plan to attempt any of these basic electrical projects, have a professional electrician inspect the work you have done before the connections are made by the professional.

The new wiring in your home will have to comply with your community's electrical codes. The store personnel where you purchase electrical supplies should know the codes. If not, check the building administration in your town; the officials will advise you of code requirements. If your new wiring is extensive, you probably will have to obtain a building permit or wiring permit from this department.

Before purchasing electrical merchandise, familiarize yourself with the basic terminology dealing with electricity.

Current

There are two types of current: alternating current (AC) and direct current (DC). Your home probably is supplied with alternating current. AC is a flow of electricity that reverses its direction at regularly recurring intervals, usually 60 cycles per second. Direct current, or DC, usually is supplied from a battery or generator. This current goes directly from the power source to the object being powered.

Voltage

Voltage is an electrical force or pressure by which the electricity flows through the conductors. This force is measured in volts. Your home probably has a 240-volt system.

Ampere

An ampere is a unit of electrical current. New appliances available for kitchen remodeling, for example, are rated in amperes or "amps," and the equipment is limited to the amps it will accommodate.

Wire

When roughing-in the electrical system for any remodeling project, do not use any wire smaller than a No. 14 wire (the smaller the number the larger the wire). On regular 115-volt house power, a No. 14 wire accommodates a 15-amp fuse, 1750-watt capacity; a No. 12 wire takes a 20-amp fuse, 2300-watt capacity; a No. 10 wire takes a 30-amp fuse, 3500-watt capacity.

Black-covered wires (wire covered with black insulation) are considered hot wires; these wires carry the electrical power. White-covered wires are neutral. White wires conduct no electricity until the circuit is completed. *Never* connect a black wire and a white wire to each other.

Tools

The basic electrical tools you will need for remodeling include:

- Standard screwdriver with an insulated handle
- Phillips screwdriver with an insulated handle
- Wire strippers
- Nut driver set
- Electrician's pliers
- Razor knife
- Keyhole saw
- Drill or brace and bits

The total investment for these necessary tools is about $20. All of the tools may be used later for electrical and home maintenance projects.

To install a junction box for light switches and convenience outlets, first trace the outline of the box on the wall at the desired location next to a framing member. (How to find a framing member is discussed in Basic Framing/Foundation Techniques). Be as accurate as possible with the outline; the junction box will have to fit snugly into the opening cut for it.

With a razor knife, or a power saber saw, cut the hole for the junction box as shown. Make shallow cuts with the knife until you have penetrated the wallboard. The wallboard will fall down between the studs or framing members, leaving the opening for the box. If your walls are lath and plaster, drill a hole with a fairly large bit; then saw out the hole with a keyhole saw. The drilled hole lets you insert the tapered saw into the wall.

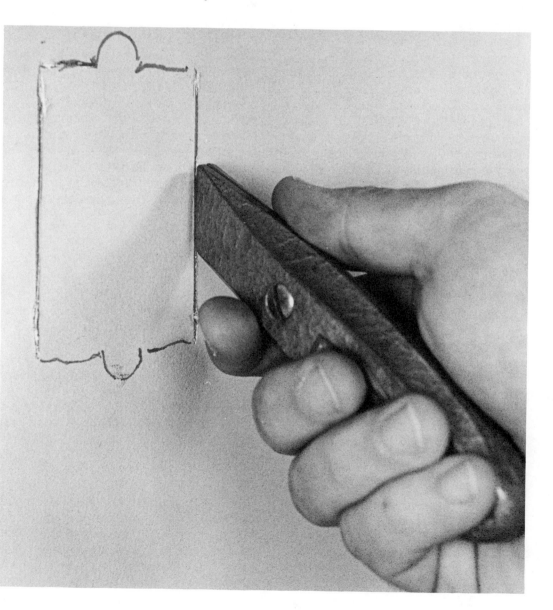

Wires for junction boxes are "fished" through the wall. Use a flexible wire with a hook on the end of it to catch the power wires. You can purchase inexpensive wire manufactured especially for fishing electrical wiring. Wiring behind old construction may take special fishing techniques. If you have an attic above, you can fish the wire down through the attic floor by drilling a hole diagonally through the supporting framing member into the wall cavity. If you do not have an attic, you will have to cut a hole in the wall near the ceiling, drill up through the framing members, and feed the wire through. You can patch the hole later.

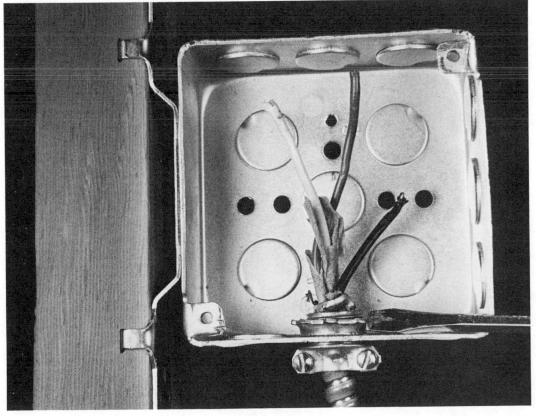

Junction boxes have knockout plugs located around the perimeter of the junction box so you can thread the wire into the box from several different angles. Punch out the plugs with a nail set and hammer; then insert the armored (sheathed in metal) cable (usually BX) and secure the cable to the junction box with a collar that screws into position. The collar is in two pieces and is called a "locknut." Turn the locknut until tight by tapping it with a hammer and an old screwdriver, as shown.

A completed junction box, whether single or double, looks like this. A mounting bracket usually goes over the front edges of a double junction box, and the bracket is especially drilled to hold the switches and/or convenience outlets. The next step is to connect the switches or outlets.

Right:

Single junction boxes are attached to studs or other framing members, if possible. If you can hook onto a framing member, special junction box brackets are available which will support the box in the wall. Use at least two small screws to fasten the box to the framing. Screws are easier to drive in tight quarters than nails. Here, an offset screwdriver is used to drive the screws.

Far right:

New plastic junction boxes are side-nailed to framing members. They may be used for behind-the-wall installation, if you have room to swing the hammer. Some junction boxes have metal prongs that secure the box to the framing. Simply tap the prongs into the framing with a hammer, as shown here. This technique works only on open framing, unless you want to remove the wallboard and patch it later.

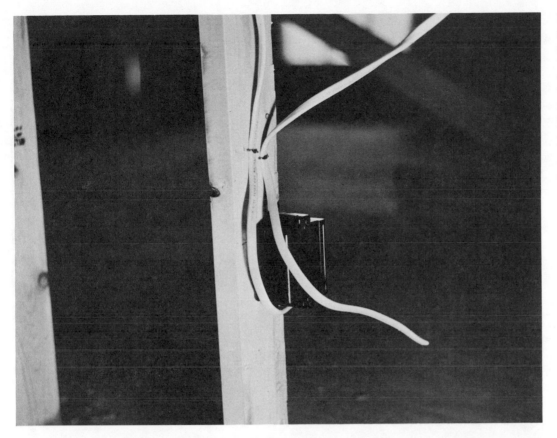

Wire is stapled to the framing members, as shown here, to hold the wire in position. Be very careful to straddle the wire with the staples and not to drive the staple points into the wire. For armored cable, special U-shaped brackets are used to secure the cable to the framing.

Wiring goes over or under windows and over doors as shown here. Drill holes in the framing, and thread the wiring through the holes. Make the holes as small as possible to accommodate the wiring, and drill in the center of the framing. In this way, the holes will not "weaken" the supporting members.

There are two types of cable recommended for indoor wiring depending on local building codes: plastic-sheathed cable and armored cable (BX). Plastic-sheathed cable may be used for both interior and exterior wiring. This cable has two solid wires which are easy to strip. BX cable is for indoor use only where there is neither water nor high humidity. BX must be used with metal junction boxes. To cut BX cable, use a hacksaw, running the saw blade across the fat part of the metal spiral. Hold the cable so it is slightly looped. When the saw penetrates the metal, bend the cable back to break it. Do not cut the wires inside the cable.

With wire strippers or a razor knife, strip away the insulation around the wires, as shown. About 1 inch of exposed wire is enough for regular connections. You should have about 6 inches of wire extending from the cut end of the armored cable. Remove the paper insulation inside the cable. Examine the insulation on the remaining 5 inches of wire extending from the cable housing. If you find a crack or break in the insulation, recut the cable and start again.

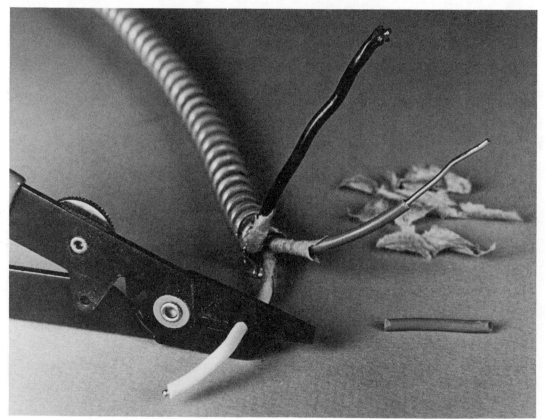

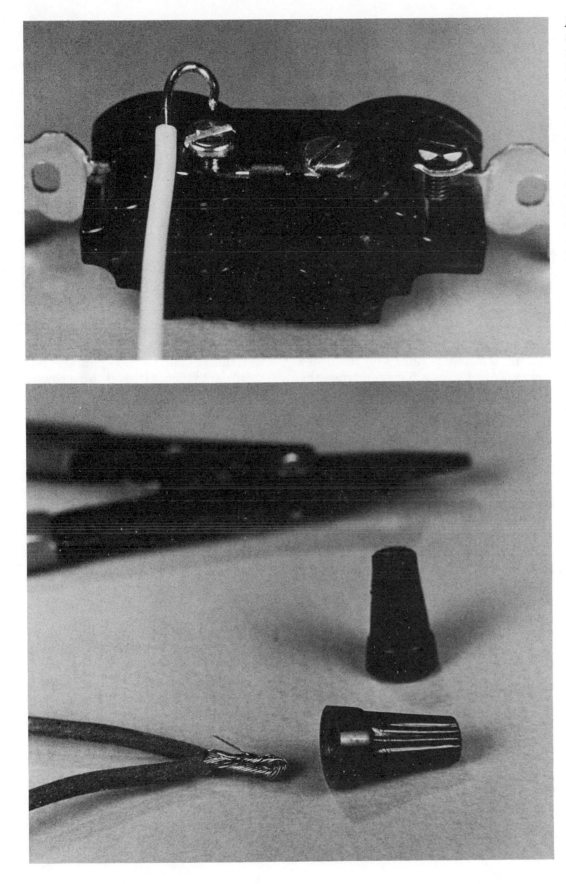

Form a loop in the bare wire, as shown. Then connect the bare wire to the switch or outlet so the wire loop goes around the terminal in the direction the screw turns— clockwise. This will tighten the wire on the terminals as the screws are turned down. Always connect the black wire to the brass colored terminal. Attach the white wire to the white terminal. Some outlets and switches have a green grounding screw. If this is the case, attach the red or green grounding wire to the green or red terminal, or directly to the junction box with a screw, which is usually provided.

Most lighting fixtures are prewired. This means you simply have to connect the power wires to the wires on the fixture— black to black, white to white. You may cover the wire with plastic electricians' tape. A better way to connect the wires is with wire nuts, as shown here. These devices simply "screw" onto the wires after the wires have been twisted together. To install a ceiling fixture, first mount a ceiling junction box. Thread the cable through one of the holes in the box, and fasten the cable with the locknut, as explained earlier. For connections, allow about 4 inches of wire from the cable to the fixture. Strip the wire and make the connections. The fixture usually is held by a mounting bracket that screws to the junction box. The light canopy or trim piece is installed on a pipe with a mounting nut.

Plumbing Basics

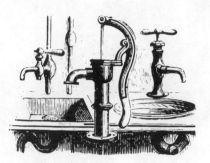

The water in your home is probably supplied by a public utility. If not, the water comes from a well or spring in the ground.

The incoming water-supply pipe divides at the hot-water heater into two separate, continuous systems: one system is for cold water and the other one is for hot water. You can trace the hot and cold water pipes starting at the hot-water heater. The hot water pipe is always on the left side of the heater; the cold water pipe is on the right. Generally, the pipes run parallel to each other throughout the house. The pressure in the pipes makes it possible for the water to flow upward in your home.

Compared to the pipes in the drainage system, water-supply pipes are relatively small. Such pipes measure anywhere from ⅜ to 1 inch inside diameter. The amount of water that comes out of the faucets in your home depends on the diameter of the supply pipe, the length of the supply pipe, and the height the water has to rise in your home. Keep these factors in mind when buying pipe for remodeling.

Installing new plumbing runs when remodeling your home is not difficult, as this chapter will illustrate. Hooking up new plumbing runs to existing plumbing is a more difficult task, and, for the most part, you should call in a professional plumber to do the job.

For those plumbing projects you plan to tackle yourself, or when attempting any plumbing in a remodeling project, there are two important rules you must follow:

1. Turn off the water at the main shutoff valve when you connect into existing plumbing. The hot and cold water pipes in your home are under pressure—usually 50 to 60 pounds per square inch. If you unscrew a coupling on an existing pipe or remove a lavatory or toilet and the water has not been turned off, you will quickly have a flood on your hands.

   Waste pipes are not under pressure; they operate on a gravity principle. The waste flows down and out of the system into the sewer (or septic tank) lines.

2. Plumbing remodeling must comply with the building and plumbing codes in your community. The dealer from whom you purchase plumbing supplies and accessories will probably know the codes. If he does not, check the city building department, city hall, or the county courthouse for the information.

Tools

For basic plumbing remodeling jobs, you will need the following tools:

4-inch adjustable wrench
Standard blade screwdriver
Phillips screwdriver
Slip-joint pliers
Solder and flux (for copper tubing)
Two 10-inch pipe wrenches

Propane torch (for copper runs)

Tube cutter (for copper)

Joint compound (for galvanized steel pipe)

The total cost for these tools should run around $50. For cutting threads on galvanized pipe or for flaring copper tubing for compression-type fittings, it is best to rent the proper equipment since the cost of these tools may be prohibitive if you plan to use them only one or two times. The equipment includes a vise, threading dies, and flaring block.

Terminology

When dealing with a plumbing supply store, a professional plumber, or even a manufacturer's instruction booklet, there are several plumbing terms you should know which can save you time and money.

Branches are hot or cold water pipes or waste pipes that are connected to the various fixtures.

Fixtures are lavatories, toilets, sinks, bathtubs, and showers to which fittings (faucets, valves, traps) are connected.

Sewer main is the big pipe that funnels the waste from your home to the city disposal plant or to the septic system.

Risers are supply pipes that extend to the second or third floor of your home (higher if you live in a high-rise building).

Valves are faucets or shutoff valves.

Remodeling with galvanized steel pipe

Galvanized steel pipe or cast-iron and threaded steel pipes are used for stacks, drains and sewers, and drains buried underground. They are also used for water-supply runs.

Galvanized steel pipe is a quality product. As a rule, you can purchase steel pipe that is threaded at both ends; it is fairly easy to assemble since the joints are simply screwed together. The pipe is available in a wide range of lengths and sizes which

means you do not have to buy—or rent—threading equipment, except for specialized jobs.

Most drainage systems are designed using cast-iron pipe and fittings for all main stacks, any toilet branch drain, the house drain, and for any pipe branch that is buried either underground or in concrete. Cast-iron pipe and fittings are available in 2-, 3-, and 4-inch sizes; pipe, in 5- and 10-foot lengths.

The plumbing system in your home looks something like this. The hot and cold water pipes are continuous and join at the hot-water heater. Since the hot and cold waters are under pressure, the pipes may be horizontal or vertical. Drainage pipes, which are not under pressure, have a slight downward pitch to take advantage of the pull of gravity.

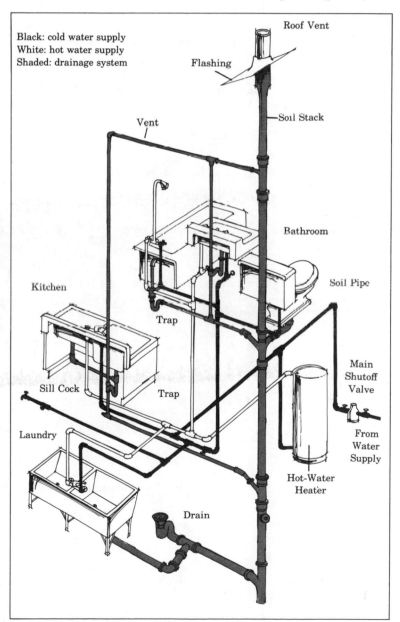

Black: cold water supply
White: hot water supply
Shaded: drainage system

Roof Vent

Flashing

Vent

Soil Stack

Bathroom

Kitchen

Soil Pipe

Trap

Main Shutoff Valve

Sill Cock

Trap

From Water Supply

Laundry

Hot-Water Heater

Drain

Galvanized steel pipe and fittings are used for all other parts of the drainage system, including secondary soil stacks, vent lines joining a stack, and branch drains other than those listed under cast-iron pipes. Galvanized steel pipe and fittings are available in 1½- to 2-inch sizes; pipe, in 10-foot lengths.

"Sanitary" drainage fittings, designed especially to avoid any solid accumulation in the pipes, are used in all drainage lines that carry waste water. All cast-iron fittings are "sanitary" type.

"Standard" (non-sanitary) and "regular" (non-sanitary) threaded fittings are used in vent fittings where only gases are carried. Galvanized steel fittings are available in both the sanitary and standard types.

Regular galvanized steel pipe and fittings are mainly used in water-supply systems, particularly in areas where pipes may be subject to damage; galvanized pipes resist shocks and blows. These pipes are available in standard sizes of ½, ¾, and 1 inch and in pipe lengths up to 21 feet. Pipe lengths are available already threaded, and the fittings are similar to those used in drainage systems.

Depending on the building codes in your area, you may be able to use plastic pipe or fiber pipe for drainage systems. You also may be able to use plastic pipe for cold water systems. Copper and clay pipe may be used for drainage as well as water systems.

Pipe length is measured from the face edge of one fitting to the face edge of the other fitting. The length of the pipe that will go into the fittings at both ends is added to the basic length of the pipe.

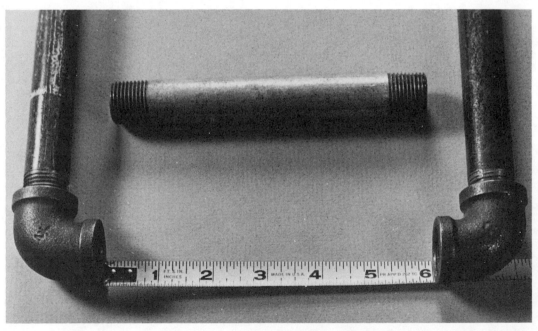

Distance Pipe Goes into Standard Fittings

Size of pipe	Distance into fittings
½ inch	½ inch
¾ inch	½ inch
1 inch	9/16 inch
1¼ inch	5/8 inch
1½ inch	5/8 inch
2 inches	11/16 inch

Pipe joint compound, or a plastic-type tape made for this purpose, is always used when you assemble galvanized steel pipe runs. The compound, or tape, helps prevent the joint from leaking. Apply the compound to external (male) threads sparingly. Never apply compound to internal (female) threads. Keep the compound out of the inside of the pipe so the compound doesn't block the passage.

When connecting pipe runs where couplings or fittings are involved, put one wrench on the fitting and another wrench on the pipe. The jaws of the wrenches should face in opposite directions. This helps prevent strain on the pipe and fittings when pressure is applied by the wrenches. Pipe wrenches are so powerful they can crush the walls of galvanized steel pipe and fittings. Be careful; do not overtighten the fittings.

A *union fitting* is a must in fabricating galvanized steel pipe runs. The unions must be installed where you cut through a pipe or where you add a pipe. Standard fittings turn one way; union fittings turn in opposite directions so the plumbing run can be completed. Always match thread size to the prethreaded pipe when purchasing pipe and fittings. Drain fittings (sanitary) are smooth inside. Standard fittings (non-sanitary) are used in vent systems only. Plastic, bronze, copper, and brass fittings are for water-supply lines only.

To add a new pipe run to an old run, it is not always necessary to dismantle the plumbing. Purchase an adapter called a "saddle tee"—shown here—that clamps around the existing pipe run. The adapter has a gasket that seals the joint. To use the adapter, turn off the water; then drill a hole through the existing pipe, inserting the drill bit into the opening in the adapter. Hook on the new pipe.

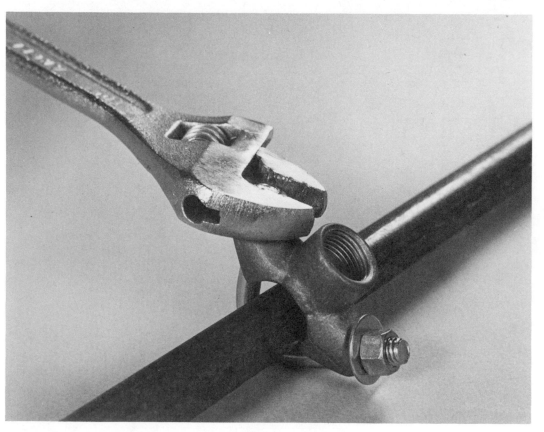

Hub-and-Spigot Cast-Iron Pipe and Fittings

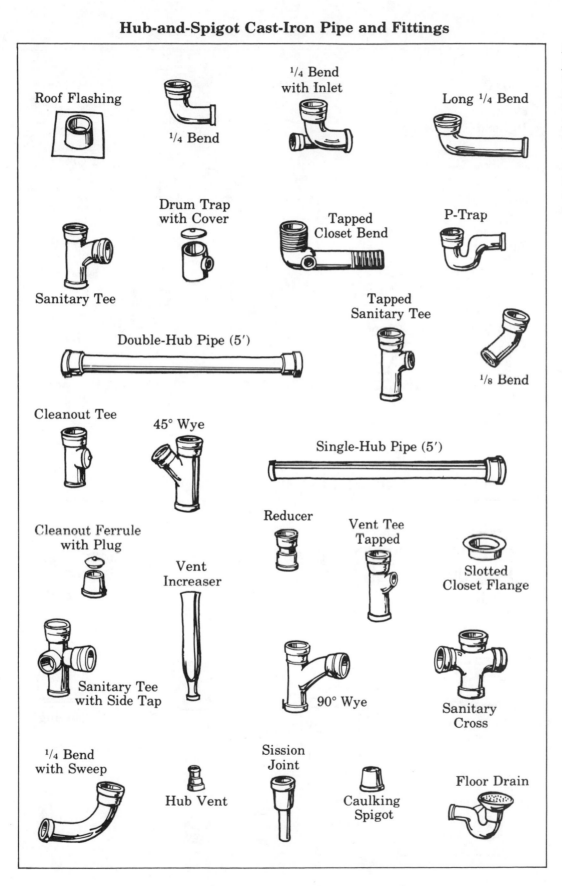

Roof Flashing

¹/₄ Bend

¹/₄ Bend with Inlet

Long ¹/₄ Bend

Sanitary Tee

Drum Trap with Cover

Tapped Closet Bend

P-Trap

Double-Hub Pipe (5′)

Tapped Sanitary Tee

¹/₈ Bend

Cleanout Tee

45° Wye

Single-Hub Pipe (5′)

Cleanout Ferrule with Plug

Vent Increaser

Reducer

Vent Tee Tapped

Slotted Closet Flange

Sanitary Tee with Side Tap

90° Wye

Sanitary Cross

¹/₄ Bend with Sweep

Hub Vent

Sission Joint

Caulking Spigot

Floor Drain

Hub-and-spigot cast-iron pipe and fittings are connected by inserting a spigot end into a hub end and then caulking the joint. (The words "tap" and "tapped" used in identifying some of the fittings mean that the particular fitting has a threaded opening for a steel pipe connection).

No-Hub Cast-Iron Pipe and Fittings

No-hub cast-iron pipe and fittings are easily connected by the use of special sleeve couplings.

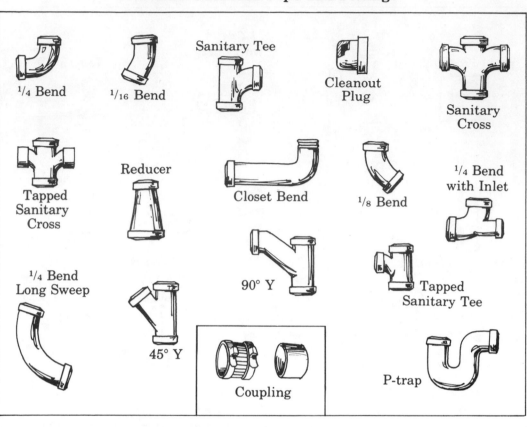

1/4 Bend

1/16 Bend

Sanitary Tee

Cleanout Plug

Sanitary Cross

Tapped Sanitary Cross

Reducer

Closet Bend

1/8 Bend

1/4 Bend with Inlet

1/4 Bend Long Sweep

45° Y

90° Y

Tapped Sanitary Tee

Coupling

P-trap

Standard Steel Pipe Fittings

Steel pipe and fittings are connected by screwing an externally (male) threaded end into an internally (female) threaded fitting.

Tee

90° Ell

45° Ell

90° Street Ell

Reducing Tee

Union

Reducer

Coupling

Hose Adapter

Bushing

Plug

Cap

Remodeling with cast-iron pipe

Cast-iron pipe is probably the most popular material for construction of soil and waste stacks. The pipe has a bell-shaped "hub" at one end; the other end is rigid and termed a "spigot." The spigot end fits into the hub.

You can also purchase cast-iron pipe with no-hub joints. Such pipe is easier to work with than hub-and-spigot pipe since neoprene gaskets are used at the joints instead of lead, caulking, and oakum. The gaskets permit slight variations in alignment, so you don't have to align each piece perfectly. There also is less wasted pipe length with no-hub pipe.

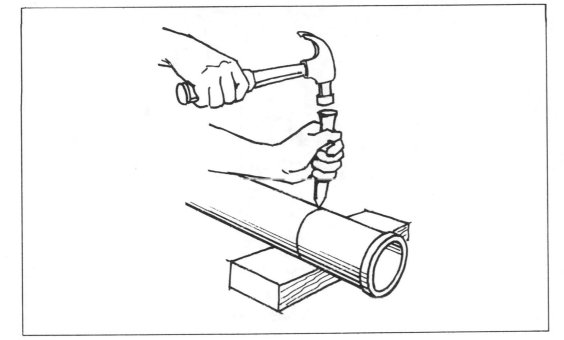

To cut cast-iron pipe, mark a cutting line on the pipe. Use a hacksaw to make a saw kerf (groove) at the mark about $\frac{1}{16}$ inch deep. Turn the pipe to complete the kerf all around the pipe. Lay the pipe on a 2- by 6-inch board. Use a cold chisel and hammer to tap around the groove. Pound lightly, going completely around the pipe. Continue this process until the pipe breaks.

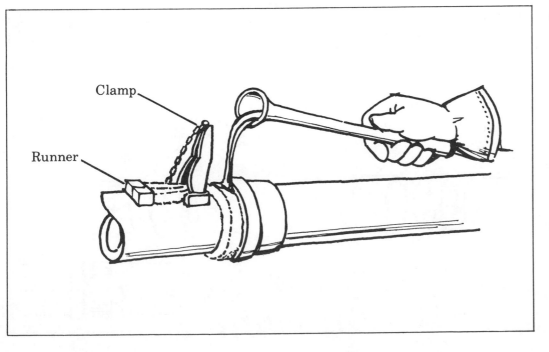

Clamp

Runner

Make horizontal joints in a vertical position, if possible. This can be done with short lengths of cast-iron pipe. If the joint must be made in the horizontal position, you will have to have a joint runner to prevent the molten lead from spilling out of the joint as the lead is poured. Clamp the pliable runner around the spigot end of the pipe and up against the hub. This seals the pipe so that you can fill the pipe with hot lead.

Right:

To assemble a vertical joint with cast-iron pipe, assemble the pipe and pack the hub with oakum. The depth of the oakum should be about 1 inch from the top of the hub.

Far right:

Fill the hub with molten lead. It takes about 1 1/2 pounds of lead to fill a 2-inch pipe joint. The lead should be just hot enough to pour, but not hot enough to burn the oakum.

Caulk the joint once the lead has cooled. The caulk should be uniform and tightly packed. Do not hammer too hard to pack it in; you might crack the joint.

Right:

No-hub pipe joints are made with special sleeve couplings. Slip one end of the sleeve over the pipe as far as it will go. Put the stainless steel shield with clamps around the other end of the pipe.

Far right:

Push the second pipe end into the sleeve as far as it will go; the pipe ends should be tightly butted together. Slide the metal shield to the center of the sleeve coupling and tighten the two clamps with a torque wrench set to release 60 pounds. Fittings are joined in exactly the same manner as straight joints. Adapters are available for fitting no-hub pipe to other pipes.

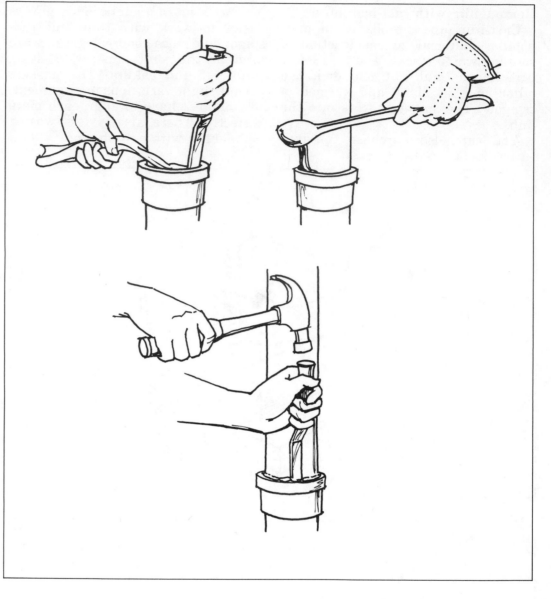

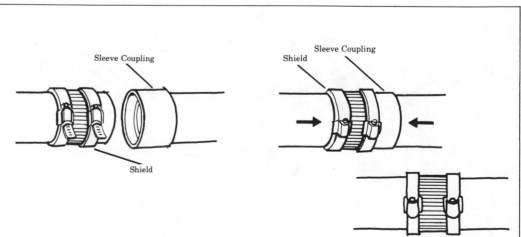

Sleeve Coupling

Shield

Sleeve Coupling

Shield

Remodeling with copper pipe and tubing

Copper pipe and tubing have two big advantages: they are lightweight and do not have to be threaded at the joints.

The pipe and tubing are manufactured in both rigid and flexible lengths, both of which resist corrosion and are quite durable.

Like any other plumbing project, check your local plumbing codes before using copper pipe or tubing.

Copper pipe is available in three weights:

1. Type *K*—thick-walled
2. Type *L*—medium-walled
3. Type *M*—thin-walled

Type K copper tubing is usually permitted for use underground. Type L tubing may be used for any residential plumbing. Type M tubing is for waste or drainage lines. However, it takes a lot of heat to join the type M material together.

Rigid copper pipe is probably easier to work with than its flexible cousin because the joints are always straight. But flexible copper tubing is better used for vertical installations where you must thread the pipe through a wall or ceiling.

Copper pipe and tubing are easily assembled "dry" before making any solid, permanent connections. This feature can be a great advantage to you, saving time and money in wasted materials—especially if you have made errors in your layout calculations. Before buying any materials, first determine the type joining techniques you will be using: sweat-soldered joints, flared joints, or compression joints.

Copper Fittings

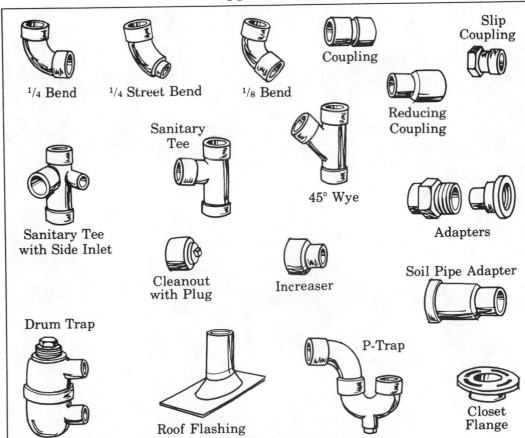

1/4 Bend

1/4 Street Bend

1/8 Bend

Coupling

Slip Coupling

Reducing Coupling

Sanitary Tee

45° Wye

Adapters

Sanitary Tee with Side Inlet

Cleanout with Plug

Increaser

Soil Pipe Adapter

Drum Trap

Roof Flashing

P-Trap

Closet Flange

Tools for working with copper pipe and tubing are fairly inexpensive, but the type of tools you choose should depend on the joining techniques your job requires. For example, if the job dictates sweat-soldered joints, you do not need to buy a flaring tool.

For both copper pipe and tubing you will need a hacksaw or a tube cutter. You will also need a propane torch if the joints are to be sweat-soldered, as opposed to flared or compression fittings. If the joints are to be flared, you will need a flaring block and flaring tool. There is a flaring tool that may be driven with a hammer, but this technique can be risky since you must hit the tool squarely with the hammer. Any mistakes could cause the pipes to leak.

If the joints are to be compression fittings, you will need a set of adjustable wrenches. Flared joints and compression joints are similar in assembly. However, compression joints are slightly more expensive to make than flared joints.

Other necessary materials include steel wool, soldering flux, and a spring tube bender if the tubing will need to be bent. If only slight bends are required, you can make the bends by pulling the tubing down over your knee. Be careful not to kink or bend the tubing at right angles. A good rule to follow: the larger the diameter of the tubing, the less you are able to bend it; large diameter tubing tends to kink.

A copper tube cutter handles sizes up to 1½ inches in diameter. For larger sizes, use a fine-toothed hacksaw. The inexpensive tube cutter has a cutting wheel. Rotate the wheel around the tubing. After every two circles, tighten the thumbscrew, which applies more pressure to the cutting wheel. If you use a hacksaw to make the tubing cuts on larger pipes, make sure the saw is square on the tubing.

Smooth rough edges of the tubing where you cut it with a file. File the inside of the pipe as well as the outside. All burrs must be removed so that the pipe will fit snugly into the hub of the fitting. The inside of the fitting hub must also be unmarred and perfectly clean.

Shine the ends of the tubing with fine steel wool until they sparkle. The steel wool removes all grease from the copper so that the solder and flux can form a good bond. Any dirt, moisture, or oil from your hands will prevent a good weld. Check the end of the pipe where it goes into the fitting; the end must be square and free from burrs and nicks. Prefit the connections, making sure they fit tightly.

Apply soldering flux evenly to the end of the tubing after it is properly cleaned. Apply the flux to the inside wall of the fittings as well. Flux is used to make the solder flow more evenly and to prevent the heat from a propane torch from oxidizing the copper. Use only non-corrosive flux; do not use acid flux on copper materials.

Use solid-core wire solder, never soft-core solder. The best solder to use for copper joints is "50-50" wire solder—50 percent lead, 50 percent tin. It flows at 250° F. and is slow to harden. To assemble copper joints, first insert one end of the pipe into the fitting. Heat the joint with a propane torch, using just the tip of the flame (the tip is the hottest point). When the fitting reaches soldering temperature (test it by touching with solder), apply the solder to the joint. The solder will form a tiny fillet around the shoulder of the fitting. Keep the flame evenly distributed on the fitting and the pipe, and do not overheat the metal.

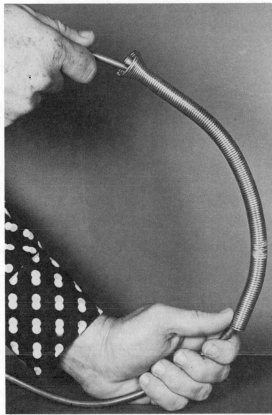

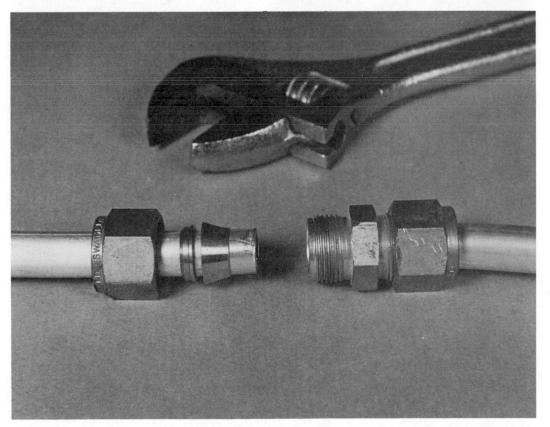

Far left:
The completed joint connection should be full of solder—no gaps around the shoulder of the joint. When you make any repairs on copper tubing water systems, be sure to drain the pipes after you turn off the water. Copper tubing *must* be dry when you work with it. If it is not, the solder will not adhere properly to the metal. If it becomes necessary to break a joint for repairs, heat the joint and pull it apart—after you turn off the water.

Left:
Bend copper tubing with a special springlike tube bender. Insert the tubing into the bender, turning the tubing clockwise as you push it in. The tubing should protrude beyond the point where you want the bend. Bend the tubing and spring over your knee.

Flexible copper tubing may be assembled with compression joints and fittings. Or you may solder it to the joints as described earlier. Slide compression fittings onto the tubing; then assemble the joint with a screw fitting as shown here. The advantage of using compression fittings (and flare joints) is the flexibility of working with the copper and the fact that the joint may be easily disassembled. Compression and flare fittings, however, are more costly than regularly soldered joints.

Remodeling with plastic pipe and tubing

Rigid plastic pipe is an easy product to work with; it is lightweight, and the joints fit together like a child's toy building set. If you make a mistake in measurement, the pipe is easy to disassemble.

There are three types of plastic pipe used for home plumbing:

1. PVC (polyvinyl chloride)
2. CPVC (chlorinated polyvinyl chloride)
3. ABS (acrylo-mitrile butadiene-styrene)

All three types of rigid plastic pipe may be used in the cold water-supply system. Only CPVC pipe can be used in the hot water-supply system and your home's drainage system.

CPVC pipe is usually available in ½- and ¾-inch sizes. For hot and cold water, the ½-inch size is generally specified; the ¾-inch material is used for main distribution lines. Larger sizes of rigid plastic pipe are also for main stacks, toilet branch drains, and house drains (3-inch material). Two-inch plastic pipe may be used for secondary stacks and some branch drains.

Plastic pipe ratings are stamped on the pipe in pounds per square inch (psi). The rating should match the water pressure in your city. The plumbing outlet where you purchase the pipe can supply this information.

Flexible plastic tubing is made from polyethylene. It is usually black in color and may be used for such outside projects as underground sprinkler systems, wells, and supply lines to gardens. This tubing is generally sold in 100-foot coils, and should never be used for hot water runs.

The flexible tubing is usually available in three pressure categories: the best is rated to withstand up to 125 psi. The medium-quality tubing is rated to take up to 100 psi; the utility grade is used only for low pressure installations such as sprinkler systems.

Some local codes restrict the use of plastic pipe and tubing to lawn sprinkler systems. Use of the material within or behind walls is generally forbidden. Always check the plumb-

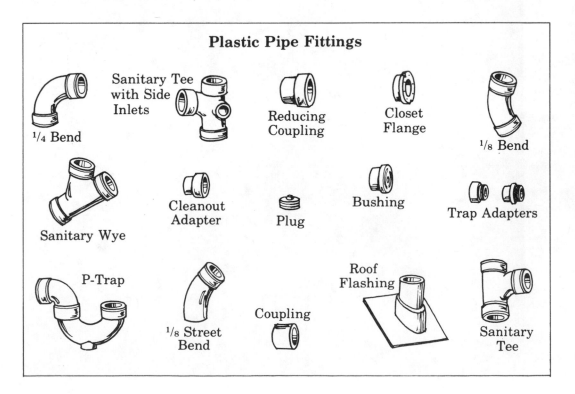

Plastic Pipe Fittings

¼ Bend

Sanitary Tee with Side Inlets

Reducing Coupling

Closet Flange

⅛ Bend

Sanitary Wye

Cleanout Adapter

Plug

Bushing

Trap Adapters

P-Trap

⅛ Street Bend

Coupling

Roof Flashing

Sanitary Tee

ing codes in your area before using the material for new or remodeled plumbing runs.

Recommendations for connecting plastic pipe to copper tubing and iron pipe are given below. When you purchase plastic pipe, be sure to ask for any available manufacturers' literature on specific procedures in making the connections. The procedures here are general. However, they apply in most installations.

When connecting plastic pipe to copper tubing, you can break a ¾- or ½-inch copper line almost anywhere in the system. Then add a take-off tee to the line, using a copper tubing adapter.

If you are connecting into an iron pipe system, try to add the plastic pipe as closely as possible to a union joint in the iron pipe. This will save plenty of time, since you can work from the union back to an existing elbow. The elbow then may be replaced with a new iron tee, and the plastic pipe connection can be made at this point.

If you have to cut a straight section of existing iron pipe, try to select a short section. You will have to replace the old iron pipe with a new section of plastic pipe. Thread the adapters onto the iron fittings, and use a tee in the center of the new pipe as a take-off for the new plastic line.

At this point you should measure the length of pipe you need. Measure along the exact line the new pipe is to follow. If you need more than one length of pipe for the run, make sure you note how many different couplings you will need for the project.

Far left:
To cut, use a hacksaw with a light forward cutting pressure. Keep the hacksaw square to the pipe so the fittings will seat properly. When fabricating long runs with plastic pipe, allow for ½-inch length of material for the fittings; use the longest length pipe possible (10 feet is standard). Example: the run is 8 feet long with two couplings. The length then should be 8 feet 1 inch. This way, you will avoid unnecessary coupling joints. Rigid plastic pipe in long runs must be supported with hangers.

Left:
Remove any burrs from inside the pipe with a knife. Simply run the cutting edge of the knife around the inside edge of the pipe. Sand the ends of the plastic pipe with fine grit abrasives. All burrs and nicks should be removed before the fittings are cemented or clamped in position. Assemble the pipe run "dry"; do not cement or clamp the fittings until you are sure that all elements fit together perfectly.

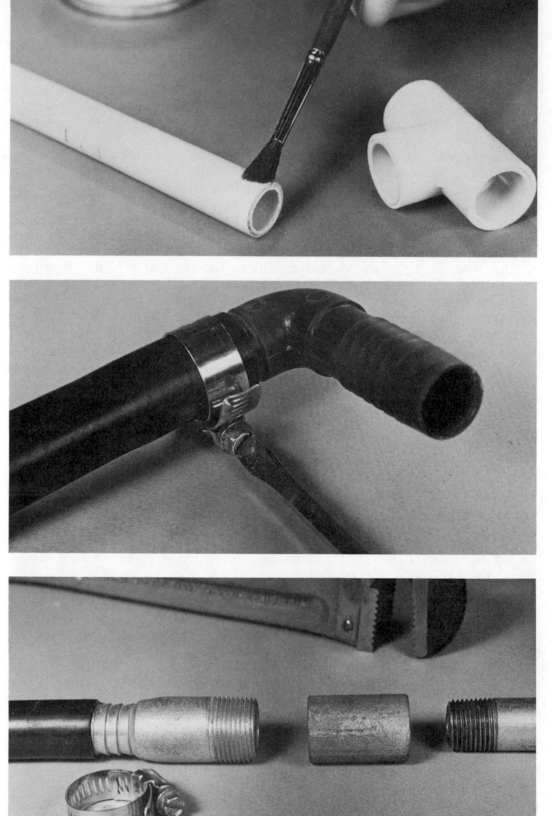

Apply the cement to the pipe with a small, artist's brush; do not stick the pipe end into the cement. Be sure to use the cement recommended only for the type of pipe you are using. Twist the fitting or coupling on the pipe, and center it in the desired position. The cement should form a tiny bead at the shoulder of the fitting or coupling. If it does not, remove the fitting and re-cement it. Once the cement is dry—and it dries quickly—you cannot remove the fitting without cutting the pipe.

Flexible plastic tubing is fastened to fittings with clamps instead of cement. Use stainless steel worm clamps, particularly when joining the tubing to nonthreaded fittings. There are many different types of fittings available; the fitting should fit the inside diameter of the tubing.

Flexible plastic pipe may be joined to steel pipe with a steel fitting and coupling, as shown. It also may be joined to itself with polystyrene fittings and couplings. If you have to disassemble a joint, pour hot water on the plastic pipe. This will soften the plastic and make it easier to break the seal by pulling the joint apart.

Planning plumbing projects

There are three basic steps in planning a plumbing project:

1. Select the proper fixtures. The first consideration is your need; the second is your budget. Plan with size, color, and styling of the fixtures in mind; you are going to live with them for some time. Also, think about the location of the fixtures in a room—bathroom, kitchen, laundry area, basement. The fixtures should be convenient and easy to use. The fixtures also should fit your life-style.

2. Estimate your plumbing needs. This involves determining the proper sizes and lengths of pipes, the types of fittings that are required for the pipes, and how and where the piping and drain connections to your present plumbing system will be made.

3. Install the plumbing. Or at least know enough about the plumbing plan in your home to help a professional plumber make the necessary changes. Check the plumbing codes in your area to make sure the piping and fixtures you plan to use meet the standards.

This section includes a potpourri of plumbing installation techniques designed to help you efficiently plan your plumbing project and to do much of the work yourself. This section is not designed to show you how to install an entire plumbing system. Rather, it is a guide to remodeling projects. The accompanying photos and drawings should help familiarize you with plumbing designs and layouts you would not ordinarily be able to see.

Far left:

Pipe runs within walls are threaded through holes drilled in the framing members with an expansion bit or hole saw. You can also notch the studs to support the pipes. Horizontal water runs must have a 1-inch downward pitch every 4 to 5 feet to keep the water flowing.

Left:

Kitchen sink hookup. The copper tubing is used for both hot and cold water supply. The plastic pipe is used for drainage.

Right:

Shower stall hookup. The hot and cold water-supply pipes connect to a diversion valve. For support, the pipes will be fastened to framing members.

Far right:

Bathtub supply lines extend into the wall. The studs are notched to recess the piping. When completed, the faucet assembly will be flush with the back of the wall.

Right:

Shower head rough-in. A piece of dimension lumber is utilized to support the riser pipe. This is about 5 feet above the subfloor. The bathtub should be correctly positioned when the framing is completed and before the piping is installed.

Far right:

Lavatory rough-in. Copper tubing is used for the hot and cold water-supply lines; plastic pipe is used for the drainage system.

Toilet assembly rough-in includes a cold water-supply pipe for the flush tank and a plastic pipe for the waste. A shutoff valve on the water-supply line should be included when the flush tank is hooked up.

Piping goes between and through joists. Shown is a plastic P-trap. If you plan to sweat-solder copper joints around wood with a propane torch, be sure to shield the wood with a piece of asbestos board. Also, with copper and plastic pipe, preassemble as much of the run as possible.

Sink and dishwasher hookup

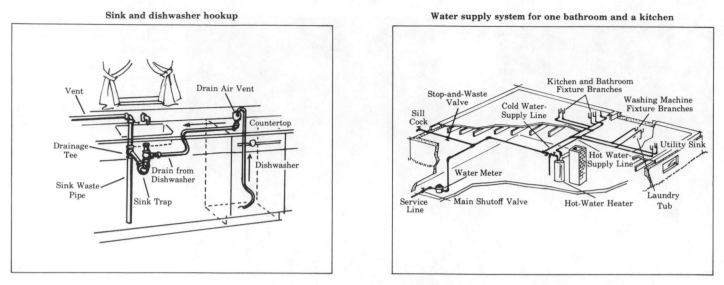

Water supply system for one bathroom and a kitchen

Running pipes through walls and floors

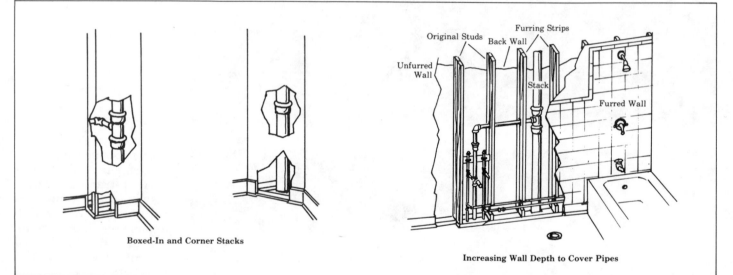

Boxed-In and Corner Stacks

Increasing Wall Depth to Cover Pipes

Framing and measurements for a lavatory

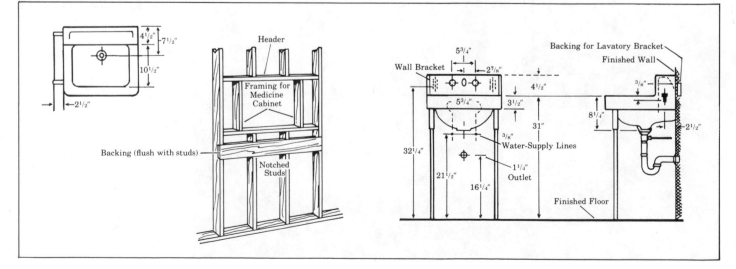

Two ways to join a new drainage system to an old one

Framing for a floor-mounted toilet

Connecting lavatory waste pipes

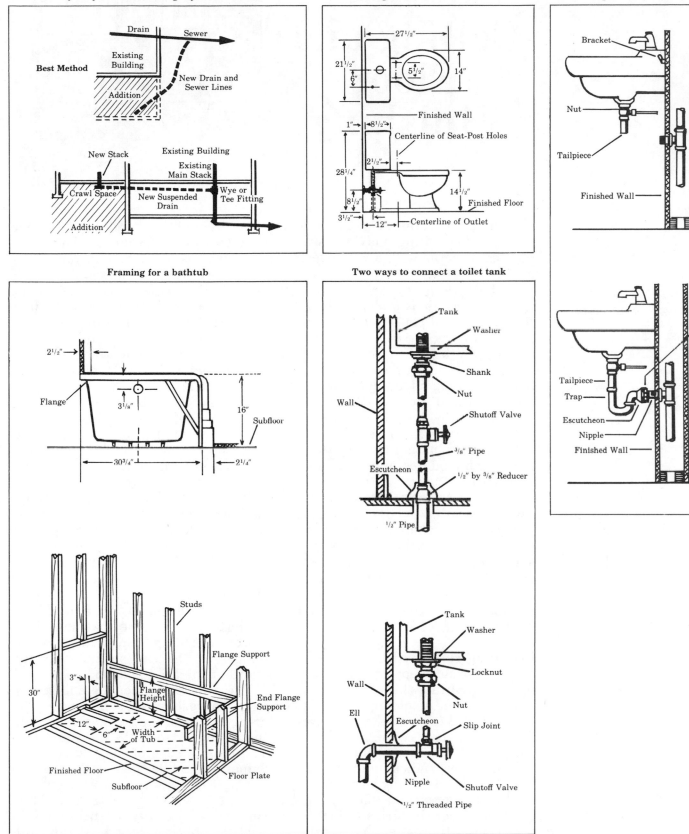

Framing for a bathtub

Two ways to connect a toilet tank

Ceiling and Floor Finishing

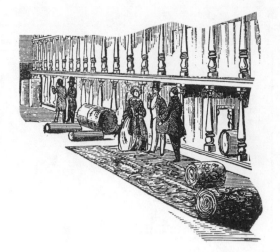

There are several ways to remodel a ceiling: the ceiling may be simply painted, covered with a wallcovering, or tiled.

If the ceiling is cracked or out of level, ceiling tile is probably the solution. To install ceiling tile, you need either furring strips or a furring channel method. The channel method is explained in this chapter since it has several big advantages, including lower cost and speed of installation.

Named by the manufacturer (Armstrong Cork Co.) as the "Integrid" furring channel method, the system accommodates either 12- by 12-inch tiles or larger 1- by 4-foot tile units. The furring strips lower the ceiling by only 2 inches.

The furring channel is made in 12-foot lengths, and the channels are designed to receive cross-tees. The tees support the tiles. Either wood or metal molding is used to finish the ceiling around the perimeter of the room.

Installing ceiling tile

Three basic steps are involved in installing ceiling tiles:

1. Nail the molding to all four walls, 2 inches below the level of the existing ceiling.
2. Install the metal furring channels perpendicular to the direction of the ceiling joists. Start 26 inches out from one side wall, and space the strips 48 inches on center thereafter. You nail the channels to the joists, using one nail every 48 inches. The channels are self-leveling; you do not need braces or shims.
3. Start the tile installation in one corner of the room. Lay the first tile on the molding, snap a cross-tee into a furring channel, and slide the cross-tee into a special slot on the leading edge of the tile.

   Go across the room: insert the tiles and the cross-tees. The tiles should butt tightly together. All supporting metal is hidden, and the ceiling produces a smooth, monolithic appearance.

If you prefer to use furring strips rather than the metal channel method, use 1- by 3-inch strips and nail them to the ceiling, perpendicular to the joists, on 16-inch centers. Nail the strips. You will need cedar shingle shims to level the furring strips. Before you do any final nailing of the strips, test the spacing with a piece of ceiling tile. The stapling flanges of the tile should split the width of the furring strip.

The tile has a tongue-and-groove joint. These joints must fit snugly. The grooved side of the tile is slipped into the tongue edge of the adjoining tile. The tongue edge of the tile is easily damaged; handle them with care.

Staple the groove edge at the corner of the exposed tongue edge to the furring strips. Use only several staples to hold the tile in position. At the wall, face-nail the tile in position using *4d* (penny) finishing nails and a tack hammer.

You also can fasten ceiling tiles directly to the ceiling surface with adhesive. The ceiling surface, however, has to be sound and level or the tile will not fit or align properly.

Lay out the ceiling with level lines. Find the center of the ceiling, both across its width and length. Snap a chalk line at these points. As you put up the ceiling, full tiles should always be parallel to these lines.

Start tiling in a corner. If you need border tiles, put these tiles up first, and fill in with full-sized tiles. Make sure your hands are clean, or wear clean gloves, when handling ceiling tiles; dirt smudges are difficult to remove. Place a walnut-sized daub of adhesive on each corner of the tile before you press the tile in position on the ceiling surface.

Nail metal or wood molding to walls 2 inches below the level of the existing ceiling. Go around all four sides of the room. The molding and tile products are available at many home center stores and building material outlets.

Far left:
Nail the metal furring channels to the ceiling. Space the first channel 26 inches out from the wall. Space the remaining channel units 4 feet apart. Nail into the ceiling every 48 inches along the length of each channel.

Left:
Cross-tees support the ceiling tile. Attach the tees by bending the sides of the channel slightly inward; then clip the tee onto the metal furring channel. The cross-tee should slide easily along the channel.

Ceiling and Floor Finishing 71

Right:

Start installing the tile in one corner of the room when all the furring channels are in position. Position the tile, snap a 4 foot cross-tee onto the furring channel, and slide the tee into the slot on the leading edge of the tile.

Far right:

Continue across the room, installing tiles and crosstees. If you have to cut a tile to finish out a row, use the leftover piece to start the next row. Cut the tile with a razor knife and make sure the cut is square. Note how all supporting members are hidden in the finished portion of the ceiling.

Right:

To lower the ceiling more than the minimum 2 inches, tiles are slipped onto suspended runners. First nail metal or wood molding to all four walls at the height you want the ceiling to be.

Position the main runners just above the molding, suspending the runners from the ceiling with wire hangers. The first runner goes 26 inches out from a sidewall. The remaining runners are placed 48 inches on center, perpendicular to the direction of the ceiling joists.

Far right:

Install the tile starting in one corner of the room. Lay the first 4 feet of tile on the molding, snap a 4 foot cross-tee onto the main runner, and slide the tee into a specially concealed slot on the leading edge of the tile.

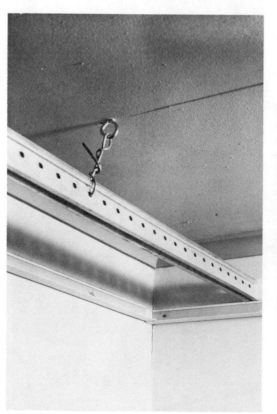

Work across the room, inserting the tiles and cross-tees. One advantage of a suspended ceiling is that it provides extra temperature and helps soundproof the room.

Floor installation basics

Besides carpeting, there are three different types of floor covering available: resilient tile, sheet vinyl, and wood strip flooring. The basic tools you will need for installing a new flooring include:

- Hammer
- Chalk line
- Carpenter's square
- Razor knife or heavy shears
- Notched adhesive spreader
- Nail set
- Small pry bar

The need for several of these tools depends on the type of floor you plan to install.

Resilient tile flooring. Resilient tile flooring is very easy to install. You can buy it with or without adhesive backing. Installation basics for self-adhesive type flooring is explained here. The very same techniques may be applied for installing floors using an adhesive and a notched adhesive spreader.

Before putting down a new floor, make sure the subsurface is smooth, clean, and dry. If the floor is painted, the paint must not be flaking, peeling, or cracking. If you are installing new flooring over an old floor covering, the old covering must be tight on the subfloor.

You may install new flooring over any old floor except asphalt or vinyl tile. If the floor is wood, replace any damaged boards, and countersink any nail pops; if the floor is in bad condition, you may have to cover it with a hardboard underlayment. Use tempered hardboard and space the joints about $\frac{1}{32}$ inch apart. This allows room for expansion and contraction of the material. Space the nails about 3 inches apart.

Sheet flooring. Sheet flooring is manufactured in continuous rolls. It is easy to install; you fasten it down with staples around the edges of a room. Or it may be nailed to the subfloor. The material is very flexible, and, in fact, can be folded like a blanket. The material has a built-in margin for error. You can trim it less than perfectly, yet obtain a perfect fit because the material will stretch somewhat.

Wooden strip flooring. Wood floors, frankly, are not easy to install. The wood is usually oak, and oak is very tough to nail. However, a wood floor is not beyond an average handyman's skills. Patience is the key word when working with the wooden strips.

Wood strip flooring comes prefinished and unfinished. We recommend that you buy the prefinished product, which will eliminate much of the work.

A wood strip floor may be laid over any smooth subfloor surface, and should be positioned to run the length of the room. Make sure all nailheads in the subflooring are countersunk before you start laying the floor.

Stagger the underlayment joints. Four corners should not meet at one point. Use ring-type nails or cement-coated nails to fasten the hardboard to the subfloor. Make sure all nailheads are driven flush with the hardboard surface. Hardboard is very dense; you may have to drill pilot holes for the nails to prevent their bending when you hammer them into the subfloor.

Remove the baseboard from the room, using an old chisel. Divide the room into quarters, and snap a chalk line at the halfway point between the long and short walls. This will mark the center of the room where you will start laying the tile. Do not guess at the center measurements; double-check them before you continue with the project.

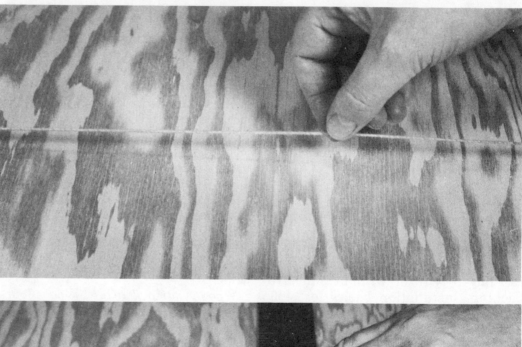

After snapping the chalk lines, check the center point for square with a carpenter's square. If the lines are not accurate, snap them again. When laying floor tile and parquet blocks, you must start on the square.

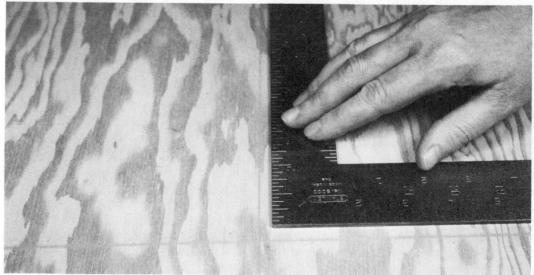

Check your measurements with tile. Lay one row of tile dry along one line and another row of tile along the other line. You may do just one quarter of the room this way, but it is best to go completely across the room in both directions. This will give you an idea of how the tile will be spaced.

If the last tile in the row at the wall is over 8 inches or under 2 inches of fitting, move the center line over 6 inches. Snap a new line. Ideally, the space between the wall and the last tile you set should be a half-tile width. By moving the center line to accomplish this, you will have even rows of tiles on the opposite sides of the room.

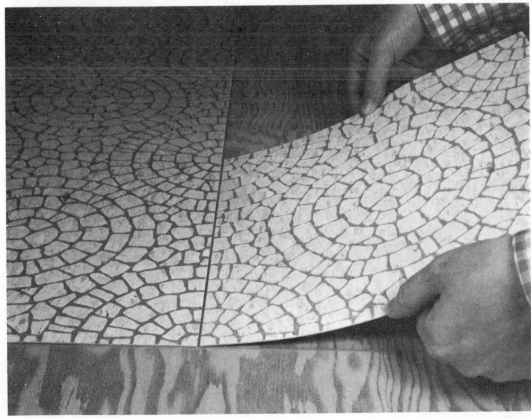

Start tiling at the center cross where the lines meet. Be very careful to set the first tile accurately; the rest of the tiles in the room will play off this center tile. If you are using self-adhesive tiles, butt each tile tightly against the next tile, as shown, making sure the pattern in the tile matches. If you are spreading the adhesive yourself with a notched trowel, do only a small area at one time.

Tile one quarter of the room at a time. Do not trim the border tiles until all the field tiles are in place. If you are using troweled adhesive, wipe off any excess adhesive that might be squeezed between the joints. Do not leave fresh adhesive on the tiles; it is very difficult to remove after it has hardened.

At the edge of the room, lay a whole tile directly over the last whole tile you set. Make sure the edges of both tiles match perfectly. You will be scribing this top tile to fit between the last tile you set and the base of the wall.

Place a second tile over the whole tile below it, and lay the second tile so it butts against the wall, as shown. The edges of this top tile must be in perfect alignment with the tile below it. Take your time and make the pattern and edges match.

Using the edge of the top tile as a straightedge, carefully draw a line on the whole tile below the top tile. Then cut the marked tile along the scribed mark. The piece you cut should fit the gap between the last whole tile you set and the wall. If you have to go around an obstruction on the floor, make a cardboard template the same size as the tile, marking the cut-out configuration. Transfer this configuration to a whole tile and make the cut with a razor knife or heavy-duty shears.

Since vinyl sheet flooring is available in widths up to 12 feet, you can put it down and not seam the material. The first step to laying this flooring is to remove the baseboard or trim pieces at the wall and floor. Make sure the floor is smooth, clean, and dry. Measure the room width and length; double-check these measurements since they have to be transferred to the vinyl sheet. In another room, unroll the vinyl sheet, and let it reach room temperature; then transfer your measurements to the sheeting. Make sure one edge of the sheet is straight, and mark on it as many cutouts as you can. In tight quarters, you may have to cut a cardboard template for irregular trim, pipes, ducts, etc. If so, transfer the measurements from the template to the vinyl, as shown.

Cut vinyl sheeting with heavy shears. Since it is already padded or cushioned, you do not need any special floor treatment. After you have cut the sheet to size, roll it up and install it. Start laying the project at the longest and straightest wall of the room. Butt the straight edge of the sheeting against the wall; then unroll the sheeting. The excess will roll up against the other walls in the room; press the sheeting in position.

Trim excess sheeting with a razor knife or heavy shears if the excess is large. At base cabinets and along walls where the molding will go, leave about ⅛ inch of excess for expansion and contraction of the material. At doorways, you should protect the edge of the sheeting with a metal strip which screws to the floor or subflooring. At the edges, the material may be nailed, stapled, or cemented to the flooring.

Apply trim moldings to complete the job. For expansion and contraction, slip a piece of fairly thin cardboard between the bottom of the trim molding and the top of the floor surface. After the molding has been fastened with either *4d* finishing nails or adhesive, remove the cardboard. If you use nails to attach the trim, drive them into the wall surface, not the floor. Countersink the nail heads, fill the holes, and paint or stain the trim.

For wooden strip flooring, space the first strip about ¼ inch from the wall surface, after you remove the baseboard or trim board at the wall and floor line. This allows for expansion and contraction of the strips after the floor has been installed.

Then snap a chalk line on the subfloor to make sure the boards are set properly. Molding will cover the gap at the wall.

Drive the flooring nails at a 45-degree angle through the tongue of the flooring; then countersink the nails with a nail set. Use 2½-inch steel-cut flooring nails to secure the floor. If the strips are fairly thin, use a 2-inch steel-cut nail. The nails do not have to be driven into the joists that support the floor.

Use a piece of scrap flooring as a buffer block when you tap the tongues and grooves together. This will protect the flooring from unsightly hammer tracks. The joints of the flooring should be as tight as you can make them. Since the flooring is tough, you may have to drill tiny pilot holes for the nails. The holes will prevent the tongues from splitting as the nails are driven into the subflooring.

Stagger the flooring joints for a neater looking floor. Do this by laying out the flooring before you nail it. This will give you an opportunity to interchange strips, stagger the joints, and match different pieces of wood. The strip flooring should be kept in the room where it will be used for about 2 days before you lay the floor.

To fill out a strip of flooring between the last long board and the wall, run the patch board against the nailed board and scribe a line at the end of the nailed strip, as shown. The patch should fit nicely between the last long board and the wall. If the strip has a tongue on the end that is to fit against the wall, cut it off; you want solid wood at the junction of the floor and the wall. Make a cardboard template at the doorways and other obstructions. Mark the flooring from the template, and cut the flooring to fit.

Face-nail the final strip to the subfloor, as shown. Face-nail the first strip as well. You may need a small pry bar to fit the last and the next to the last boards tightly together. Wedge the bar between the last strip and the wall, and apply the pressure. Have a friend face-nail the last strip while you supply tension from the prybar. The finished floor, if it is not prefinished, should have two sandings before you apply at least two coats of varnish, shellac, or polyurethane finish. After the top coat has dried, polish the finish with very fine steel wool, and wax the floor.

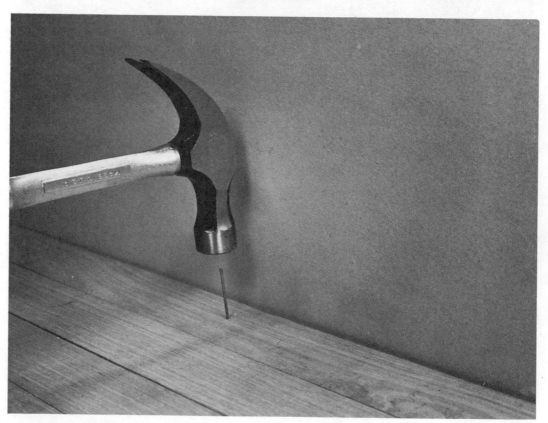

Basic Framing/ Foundation Techniques

Almost any remodeling project involves framing. The illustrations in this chapter are designed to provide you with patterns to follow when you decide to add a new room to your home, put a new door or window in your existing home, or add a new partition wall in the basement.

Most of the basic framing techniques are covered in this chapter. You may have to adapt several to fit your specific project, and this is not difficult. However, if your problem is unique, your building material retailer can probably help you.

Before you start any actual remodeling work, first draw the proposed plan—a sketch scaled to the size of the room in which the remodeling is to take place, or the size of the addition you plan to build. For this you will need a pad of ¼-inch grid graph paper. Let each square represent either 6 inches or 1 foot; 6 inch modules are best since you will be dealing with some odd measurements.

Keep the same ratio throughout the sketch, drawing in all cabinets, appliances, windows, doors, electrical outlets, etc. Once completed, the graph will give you a good idea of what goes where and why.

Most building materials come in modules—standardized widths of materials: 2, 4, 8, 10, 12, and 16 feet. By planning remodeling projects around these standard-size building modules you will save time and money; the materials will not have to be cut to a special size. You always pay for any wasted material when something has to be custom cut.

Most framing members are on 16-inch centers. One exception might be garage framing, which sometimes is put on a 24-inch center basis. Usually, the material used for framing members is dimension lumber—2 by 4s, 2 by 6s, 2 by 8s. Studs usually are 2 by 4s.

A building permit is needed before you can begin some building projects. Almost all remodeling projects have to comply with local building codes. Make sure you are in compliance with these requirements before you start pounding away. Check with local building code officials or your building material retailer to avert any future problems and to save money at the outset of your remodeling.

Prefabricated building parts

A boon to the building business over the last decade has been prefabricated building units. These include roof trusses, soffit systems, floor panels, wall panels, pre-assembled plumbing parts, pre-hung windows, pre-hung doors, cabinets, and other parts.

Such prefabricated parts can save you both time and money in a remodeling project; the job becomes one of assembly rather than nuts-and-bolts building.

Many building material outlets handle these prefabricated parts. Or, you may find the parts listed under "Prefabrication" in the yellow pages. If there is a prefabricated home builder or factory in your area, you may be able to buy parts directly from these firms.

Prefabricated parts are constructed

on modules. Therefore, if you want to take advantage of prefabrication, you will have to design your remodeling to fit the parts. For best results, work directly with the prefaber—or retain an architect who knows about prefabricated construction.

Used materials

Often you can purchase used lumber, cabinets, and building parts from a wrecking crew. Sometimes it pays to check out the materials being offered; you can find bargains. Do not be deluded by "old" looking lumber. This material usually is better than its "new" looking counterpart. You should check, however, for any defects, especially if the material has been painted.

Foundation walls

If you plan to add a room onto your home, the addition will have to sit on a foundation wall. There are two basic types of foundations: reinforced concrete and concrete blocks. When using either foundation, the bottom or footing has to be below the frost line in your area to prevent it from heaving and breaking. Determine the depth of the frost line by checking with your local building department.

Reinforced concrete foundations are really a job for a professional, since the job takes special digging equipment and forming techniques. For example, concrete forms are made of plywood locked together with metal braces and special screw hooks. The cost of this equipment would be prohibitive for a one-shot job.

A concrete block foundation may be more within your skills; the basics for this type foundation appear in this chapter. However, do not be deceived: concrete blocks are heavy and take a lot of work to set. Yet, the blocks go up fast, and the techniques of setting them are not difficult.

A concrete block foundation sits on a footing, which is below the frost line. The footing usually is reinforced concrete placed in a ditch. Specifications for this footing must come from the local building code department in your area. The type of concrete and its reinforcement will have to meet these codes. As a rule, it is best to order concrete that is already mixed for the footings.

There are two basic types of concrete block. The standard type is made from standard concrete. The standard block is heavy and dense. The light aggregate concrete block is made with lighter material, and, therefore, is easier to handle. However, local codes may dictate which type block to use.

Concrete block comes in several sizes and shapes: regular blocks, partition blocks, corner blocks, jamb blocks, and bullnose blocks. Pre-cast sills and lintels for windows are also available.

Concrete blocks are hollow. This means you can insulate the foundation wall with loose fill insulation. You can also string wiring through the hollow cores of the blocks, but the type of wire you use has to meet local codes.

Concrete blocks are held together by mortar. For a wall of standard block construction, the proportions (by volume) for the mortar is 1 part masonry cement or one part Portland cement to 2 to 3 parts loose mortar sand. If you use Portland cement, mix it 1 to 1¼ parts hydrated lime and 4 to 6 parts loose mortar sand.

For very heavy construction, use 1 part Portland cement to ¼ part hydrated lime to 2 to 3 parts mortar sand.

Tools needed to lay concrete block include these:

a mortar box (you can make one)
spirit level
hammer
brick chisel
joint strike
chalk line
mason's trowel
garden hoe
galvanized steel bucket

Far left:
Lay concrete on footings, as shown. If corners are involved, do the corners first. This will give you a base reference point for the remaining courses of block. Use plenty of mortar for the first course of block on the footings.

Left:
Block courses look like this on the footings. Once you set the base block on the mortar on the footing, do not disturb the block. The blocks should be level and plumb; check this frequently.

Far left:
Trowel mortar on the blocks, as shown. Use plenty of mortar, removing any excess with the trowel. The trick is to keep the mortar continuous throughout the wall. Do not skimp on the mortar; set about 4 blocks at a time.

Left:
Trowel mortar on the ends of the blocks using a slicing motion with the trowel—as you would butter a cracker. The entire width of the ends should be covered with mortar, as shown, for the best bond.

Right:

A concrete block wall looks like this as the blocks are laid. The chalk line is moved with each course of block; the chalk line serves as a leveling guide. You must use a level as you lay the blocks, however, so each course is level and plumb.

Far right:

Use a joint strike to smooth the mortar joints in the blocks. Strike the joints as you lay the blocks, and remove any excess mortar with the edge of the trowel. By striking the joints you make them slightly concave so the joints shed water.

Right:

Pipes within the foundation walls should be set before the walls are built. Protect the pipes from damage with a concrete block, as shown. After the walls are up, the concrete floor is placed inside the walls. Expansion strips generally are used between the footings and the floor. The expansion strips allow for expansion and contraction of the concrete.

Far right:

A completed foundation wall. The difference in the width of the blocks is to accommodate a brick veneer at the grade (ground) level. Metal tabs are inserted in the mortar lines here so the bricks may be "tied" to the concrete blocks. The space between the ground excavation and the foundation wall will be backfilled with earth.

Far left:
Foundation walls that will be below grade should be protected with a sheet of poly-film made especially for this purpose. The poly-film is held to the wall with daubs of asphalt roofing compound. The excavation is then back-filled; the earth presses tightly against the poly-film.

Left:
A *brick veneer* covers the concrete blocks as shown. Partition blocks are tied into walls with steel bars made for this purpose. Use the bars at the bottom, middle, and top of the wall; space the bars evenly in the dimension or height of the wall. The top of the wall is usually topped off with a 2- by 8-inch sill. Secure the sill to the blocks with bolts positioned in mortar in the holes in the blocks. Partition blocks are 4 inches thick; the narrow measurement provides room for heating ducts.

Solving special framing problems

Joists may be notched to accept the foundation and foundation sill. The joists are spiked to the sill for stability. The joists may sit fully on the sill (not notched), toenailed into the sill. Joists usually sit on 16-inch centers.

Right:

Wall projections—usually used to accommodate a bay window—are framed with an extension of joists across the top of the foundation wall. Subflooring (and finish flooring) goes on top of the joists. The bottom is finished with plywood to protect the joists from moisture and give the projection a "finished" look. The walls are framed with a sill, studs, top plate, etc., just like a regular wall. The window is framed with jambs, a sill, and a lintel.

Far right:

Joists joining partition walls are notched to fit a ledger strip, as shown. The joists are then spiked to a header across the partition. The ledger strip gives the joists very rigid support; the strip is usually a 1 by 4 spiked to the header.

Right:

An open ceiling—such as for a living or family room—is framed as shown. The rafters will be covered with gypsum board, which will be finished. The ridge beam is decorative and functional; it will be finished and left exposed. The ceiling in the adjoining room (background) is framed with joists on 16-inch centers.

Far right:

Pipes and ducts should go either above the joists or between them. The joists are tied off here with a cross member to support an overhead heating/cooling unit.

Far left:
If the ceiling will not be finished, duct placement is not important, although the ducts should be supported by hangers and wrapped with insulation. If the ceiling will be finished, and it is impossible to sandwich the ducts between the framing members, be sure to leave enough room in the ceiling height for a suspended ceiling.

Left:
To run ducts through existing block walls, you will have to break the blocks, as shown. Then install the ducts, and fill the space around the ducts and concrete blocks with batt insulation.

Far left:
Cover wooden sheathing with asphalt building paper. The paper is held in place with special nails, as shown. Drive the nails flush with the paper/sheathing since siding will be applied over the covering.

Left:
Fireplace walls with a window insert are framed this way. The lintel of the window is a piece of steel plate made especially for this purpose. The metal may be covered with a piece of trim sandwiched between the jamb castings. Or the metal may be painted to complement the brick.

Right:

The bottom of the window in a fireplace wall has an outside sill and an interior trim piece to match the casing finish, here, rough-sawn cedar. Insulation wool is stuffed between the sill and brick; the trim sill is fastened to the casing. The window is fixed glass between the trim pieces; the glass is set in a bed of caulking compound.

Far right:

Stud framing is nailed in a *U* configuration around adjoining partition walls, thus tieing the walls together. The studs are placed 16 inches on center and are toenailed to the bottom plate.

Right:

Keep the studs on 16-inch centers, even though the spacing may be slightly off at the corners, as shown here. The extra stud here is not really needed for wall support; it serves as a nailer for the gypsum board wallboard.

Far right:

Double the studs for door and window jambs. This provides more support for the door and window. The jambs should be perfectly plumb. If not against the wall, you can shim the jambs with a piece of cedar shingle so the jambs are plumb and supported properly.

Support door jambs on concrete floors with a block of wood, as shown. Toenail the framing members to the block, which does not have to be fastened to the floor.

Door and window headers are usually 2 by 8s supported by the inside jambs. The headers also are doubled—two pieces of 2 by 8 face-nailed together. A 2 by 4 may be used as a finish piece below the headers.

Closet framing details and special dimensions are shown here and in the drawings. The photo shows how the framing members fit with attic rafters to create the necessary closet space. Double jambs and headers are used for the door openings. (See also "Closet dimensions" illustrated in Measuring and Measurements.)

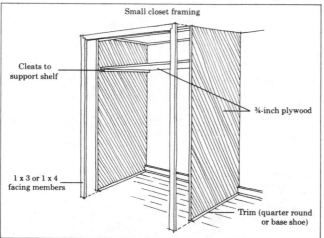

Small closet framing

Cleats to support shelf

¾-inch plywood

1 x 3 or 1 x 4 facing members

Trim (quarter round or base shoe)

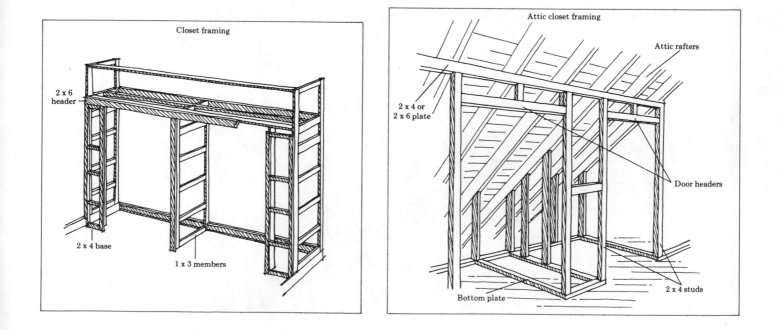

Closet framing

2 x 6 header

2 x 4 base

1 x 3 members

Attic closet framing

Attic rafters

2 x 4 or 2 x 6 plate

Door headers

2 x 4 studs

Bottom plate

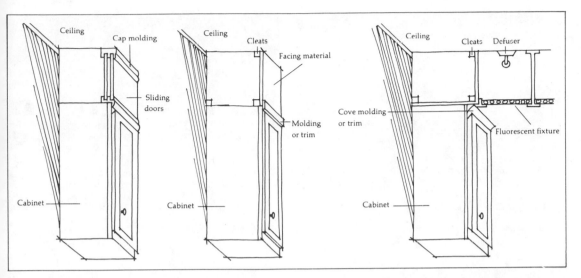

There are three different soffit treatments you can use if your plans call for a soffit over kitchen cabinets. The cleats can be 2 by 2s or 2 by 4s fastened to the ceiling, wall, and top of the cabinets. The covering can be gypsum board, plywood, glass, plastic, or tempered hardboard.

Porch and deck framing basics

Far left:

To support a deck or porch, concrete footings are needed for the support posts. Dig a hole in the ground below the frost line and fill the hole with concrete. Level the top of the concrete and center a bolt in the footing exactly where you plan to place the posts. Use 6- or 8-inch bolts, sinking all but about an inch into the wet concrete. Drill a hole in the bottom of the posts to accept the bolts, which support the posts laterally.

Left:

Framing members on a deck are spiked to the house framing members. The joists—or support members—should be 2 by 10s on 24-inch centers. The centers may depend on the width of the porch or deck. For narrow spans, only one support may be required, as shown here.

Right:

The 4 by 4 posts are notched to accept the joists or "outside" framing members of the deck or porch. Or, you can bolt the framing members to the faces of the posts. Notching is best because it provides more "sheer" support for the framing. If the house is masonry construction, you will have to drill holes for masonry anchors and lag-bolt the framing members into the anchors.

Far right:

Framing members go together in butt joints. Use heavy metal angles at the joints to add support to the joints.

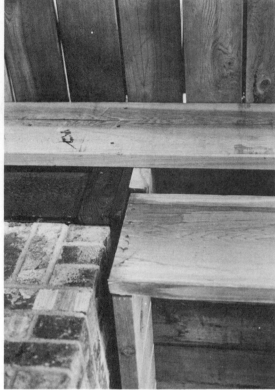

Right:

The decking is simply nailed to the joists and other framing members. Leave a small space between dissimilar materials, as shown here, to allow for expansion and contraction of the wood. You also should leave about ½-inch space between each decking board so the surface can drain properly.

Far right:

Railing support posts are nailed, lag-screwed, or bolted to the porch or deck skirting or to framing members or to the posts that support the structure. If your budget permits, use cedar, cypress, redwood, or specially treated fir lumber for decks and porches. The wood is weather-resistant; it will not rot, and it never needs painting.

Locating studs and joists behind gypsum board

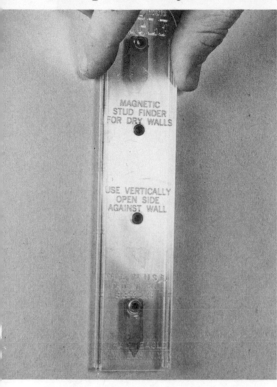

Far left:
A *magnetic stud finder,* which costs about $2, is the easiest way to locate studs in a wall or joists in a ceiling. When the finder passes over a nail, the indicators on the finders jump.

Left:
Locate the stud or rafter with a nail. Drive holes through the wall covering until you hit the stud; then mark the location on the wall. This will give you a reference point for the remaining studs or rafters. When the wall is finished after the remodeling, you can easily patch these tiny location holes with spackling compound.

Working with gypsum wallboard

Far left:
In new construction or remodeling, lap the gypsum board over the studs. If you have to cut the material to fit, score the paper covering with a sharp razor knife. Then lay the material over a 2 by 4 so that the edge of the wood follows the scored line. The wallboard will break evenly along the scored mark. Then cut the paper on the back of the board to complete the cutting job.

Left:
Use two nails on each side of the gypsum board to prevent nail pops later. Drive the nailheads flush with the wallboard; then hit the nails once more. This will leave a slight "dimple" in the surface of the wallboard, as shown. Fill the dimples with joint cement.

Spackling compound or gypsum wallboard cement is used to cement the tape into the joint. The cement is mixed to the consistency of thick whipped cream. Apply the cement to the joint with a wide wall scraper. Be liberal with the cement so the joint is completely filled.

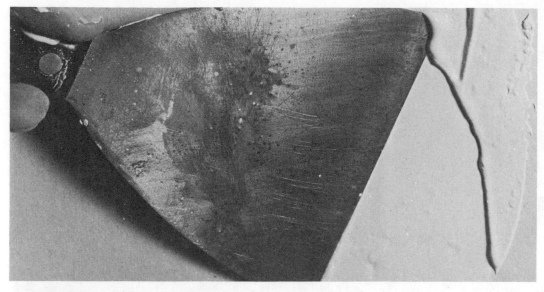

The joint tape is imbedded into the cement base. You may have to reposition the tape several times to make it smooth on the joint. For inside and outside corners, nail a metal corner molding to the gypsum board. Then cement the edges of the molding and cover with tape similar to that used on regular wallboard joints. When the tape is in position, firmly pull the scraper down the tape; this will remove any excess cement and imbed the tape properly.

Sand the joint smooth when the joint compound is dry. If you have the time, let the job set overnight. Use medium-grit sandpaper stretched over a flat sanding block. Do not dig or gouge the wall; the cement is thin and scars easily. After sanding, the wall is ready to be painted, covered with wallpaper, panels, or simulated wallcoverings, such as brick or stone.

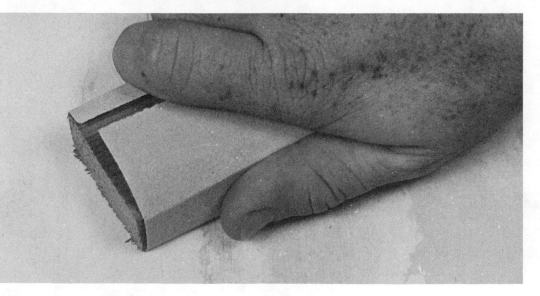

Index